# SEVEN STEPS TO GLORY

# SEVEN STEPS TO GLORY

*by*
*Frank Allred*

*Grace Publications*

GRACE PUBLICATIONS TRUST
7 Arlington Way
London EC1R 1XA
England
e-mail: AGBCSE@aol.com
www.gracepublications.co.uk

Managing Editors:
T. I. Curnow
M. J. Adams

© Grace Publications Trust

First published 2009
ISBN 10: 0 946462 78 X
ISBN 13: 978 094646 278 0

Distributed by
EVANGELICAL PRESS
Faverdale North
Darlington DL3 OPH
England

e-mail: sales@evangelicalpress.org
www.evangelicalpress.org

Printed and bound in UK by the MPG Books Group

*Thanks to my friends*
*Joanne Eaves for her meticulous*
*checking of the manuscript,*
*John Lewis and Beth Roberts*
*for their helpful comments and suggestions.*

# CONTENTS

# TO THE READER

If you have become a Christian recently, or if you are seriously interested and wanting to become one, the 'Seven Steps to Glory' are addressed to you. In this book, I assume that the reader is persuaded that God exists and that he rewards those who earnestly seek him. For this reason, I do not enter into argument about the existence or the personality of God. My sole purpose is to assist you by explaining simply how to become a Christian or, if you have already put your trust in Christ, what steps you need to take to grow in the grace and knowledge of God.

Everything I say is based on the Bible. In spite of the destructive criticism that has been levelled at the Scriptures over the years, they are still God's authentic word. The Ten Commandments are still God's standard of judgment, and the gospel is still 'the power of God for the salvation of everyone who believes' (Rom. 1:16. 'Gospel' means 'Good News').

Since there seems to be no shortage of books written to help those who are seeking the truth and those who are young in the faith, you may wonder why I have written another. The main reason is that in recent years many introductory books to the Christian faith tone down the unpalatable truths of the gospel and truths that are hard to understand, or ignore them altogether. This book will fill those gaps.

You should realise at the outset that the gospel message is not about self-fulfilment, as many think, but about saving sinners from God's wrath. It is not about happiness, but holiness.

It is not about sinners awakening the love of a dormant God, but about God fulfilling his purpose in saving sinners from eternal death. It is not exclusively about God's love, but about his judgment as well.

You may have heard the old story of the open-air preacher who danced round his hat shouting: 'It's dynamite. It's dynamite'. When a crowd had gathered, he removed his hat to reveal a Bible. No doubt, the story is fictitious, but the point is valid. The English word 'dynamite' comes from the Greek word dynamis, a word used to describe the gospel.

In English Bibles, it is translated 'power', as in the quotation above (Rom. 1:16). If vital truths are removed, however, in a vain attempt to make the gospel more acceptable, it is likely to have the opposite effect.

The gospel has always been foolish to those who consider themselves wise in the eyes of this world but do not have the wisdom that comes from God. But for millions whose lives have been transformed by the gospel, it is indeed dynamite. 'For the message of the cross is foolishness to those who are perishing, but to us who are being saved it is the power of God' (1 Cor. 1:18).

Each of the Seven Steps is essential in the life of a believer, but you should not take the order in which they are presented as inflexible. The conversion and spiritual progress of sinners varies considerably. God deals with each one differently.

For convenience, I regard the reader as male, but no discrimination is intended.

*'All over the world this gospel is bearing fruit and growing...'*
*(Col. 1:6)*

# STEP 1:
# HUMBLE YOURSELF

*'God opposes the proud but gives grace to the humble'*
*(1 Peter 5:5)*

People of high rank used to ride on high horses. This gave rise to the idea that to be on your high horse is to be proud and unteachable. It may sound rather impertinent to say that the first step to glory is to get off your high horse. Sadly, we are all handicapped by a measure of pride in this matter. By nature, we do not have that teachable spirit that is so necessary if we are to find our way to heaven. 'The Lord detests all the proud of heart' (Prov. 16:5).

Wisdom acquired in this world will not help you. It may serve a purpose in other quests, but not this one. Indeed, it could act as a barrier to your progress. The wisdom you need to understand the gospel and to live for the glory of God comes from him alone.

You must therefore, from the very beginning, ask God to give you wisdom from above, freely acknowledging that you don't deserve it (James 1:5). Only then will you gain the courage to face up to the truth about yourself. God will open your mind to understand what the Bible says about you. Indeed, everything you need to know will be found there.

*'Humble yourselves, therefore, under God's mighty hand,*
*that he may lift you up in due time'*
*(1 Peter 5:6)*

## Sink Your Pride

*'Pride goes before destruction…'*
*(Prov. 16:18)*

I have a childhood memory of a picture in a book. It was a black and white drawing of a young man, dressed in top hat and tails, strutting down a wide imposing staircase. With his nose in the air, he was putting on a pair of black silk gloves. On the next step below him, someone had left a dustpan and brush. Underneath the picture were the words: 'Pride goes before a fall'. What happened next was left to my fertile imagination. I vividly remember having a sense of satisfaction as I visualised the man crashing head over heels to the bottom of the stairs. It never occurred to me that I might have been looking at a picture of myself!

You may take comfort from the fact that there are many people out there whose pride is more odious to God than yours. We can all compare ourselves with people whose arrogance knows no bounds. It is a common failing. But there is no future in it. If you really want to find your way to heaven, you must compare yourself with the standard God sets. Knowing what *he* thinks about *you* will focus your mind. 'Man looks at the outward appearance, but the LORD looks at the heart' (1 Sam. 16:7).

I guess you, like me, think of heaven as 'up' and hell as 'down'. The Bible encourages us to think so. Similarly, pride is thought of as being haughty and humility as being lowly. Now since humbling ourselves before God is the first step to glory, we immediately arrive at an apparent contradiction: Initially, the way up is down! For if we will not humble ourselves we shall never know the way to heaven. Like it or not, like the proud man in the picture, we shall come crashing down.

This is an unchanging principle, taught by Jesus himself: 'For whoever exalts himself will be humbled, and whoever humbles himself will be exalted' (Matt. 23:12). The apostle James echoes the Lord's words: 'Humble yourselves before the Lord, and he will lift you up' (James 4:10).

Jesus told a parable about a proud religious Pharisee and a despised tax collector to illustrate this principle. (Tax collectors worked on behalf of the Roman occupying power and were not averse to a little fraudulent dealing. Therefore, they were not regarded as respectable members of society.) The two men went to the temple to pray. The Pharisee was really on his high horse. In his 'prayer' he recited his 'goodness' to God: 'God, I thank you that I am not like all other men — robbers, evildoers, adulterers — or even like this tax collector. I fast twice a week and give a tenth of all I get.' The tax collector stood at a distance and would not look up to heaven. Instead, he beat his breast and said, 'God, have mercy on me, a sinner' (Luke 18:9-14).

The verdict of Jesus on the two men shatters all human hopes of gaining God's favour by our own imagined goodness: 'I tell you that this man (the tax collector), rather than the other, went home justified before God.' The tax collector went home rejoicing in a new and right relationship with God, but not the self-righteous Pharisee.

Of course, it is not always the proud religious person who looks down on others. These days it is more likely to be the proud irreligious person who despises those who are serious about their faith. But pride is a sin, whether it resides in the heart of religious people or irreligious. If you want to make progress in the Christian life, you must ask the Lord, as a matter of priority, to make you and keep you humble.

If your heart is proud, you will never know how gracious the Lord is, because he 'opposes the proud but gives grace to the humble' (James 4:6). Whether you are seeking the truth, or have already put your trust in Christ, a proud heart will block your progress. Always remember this: the LORD hates pride (Prov. 8:13).

*'A man's pride brings him low'*
*(Prov. 29:23)*

☙

## Abandon Human Wisdom

*'For the wisdom of this world is foolishness in God's sight'*
*(1 Cor. 3:19)*

Did you know that the wisdom tooth is so named because it appears in the late teens or early twenties, when its owner is assumed to have reached the age of discretion? When I see young men of this age driving their old cars past my home at crazy speeds, I have cause to question the assumption. Not much discretion here! Nevertheless, the general principle — that we learn wisdom with the passing of the years — is true.

Wisdom acquired in this way is not to be despised, if properly used. An example of its fraudulent use is seen in the parable of the Unjust Steward (Luke 16:1-13). After his boss had given him the sack, the ex-steward enriched himself by accepting drastically reduced payments from his former employer's debtors and pocketed the cash. Obviously, the boss did not like it, but he had to acknowledge the cunning of his former manager.

At the end of the parable, Jesus told his disciples that 'the people of this world are more shrewd in dealing with their own kind than are the people of light'. He was not approving of dishonesty, but pointing out that worldly people are usually more astute in worldly affairs than Christians are in spiritual matters. Godless people are more eager to benefit from their association with people of their kind than believers are from their kind.

Believers who are eager to use every opportunity to promote their knowledge and their spiritual well-being are exceptions to this rule. They are diligent in their Bible-reading and prayer. They benefit more than others do from worship and fellowship. They put God first in their families and business affairs. Just as the hard work of worldly people brings prosperity, so the diligence of believers pays dividends in terms of assurance, usefulness and joy.

So what does God think about worldly wisdom? Does he regard it as a useful tool in the search for truth? Does he see it as necessary to our spiritual health and growth? Not at all. On the contrary, he sees it as foolishness! 'For the wisdom of this world is foolishness in God's sight' (1 Cor. 3:19). In your quest to find your way to heaven, you must set your human wisdom aside. It may be of value in the affairs of this world when used with integrity, but it is useless when it comes to knowing God.

Paul, the apostle has some good advice for you in this matter: 'Do not deceive yourselves. If any one of you thinks he is wise by the standards of this age, he should become a "fool" so that he may become wise' (1 Cor. 3:18). Be clear in your mind that no one has the wisdom to know the way to heaven unless God reveals it to him. No matter how much worldly wisdom we have, we are, by nature, both ignorant and helpless when it comes to knowing God.

It stands to reason that if wisdom acquired in this world were of value in finding the way to heaven, some people would have a considerable advantage. But in his wisdom, God has decreed that worldly wisdom shall give advantage to no one. On the contrary, it will act as a barrier, because to the worldly wise, God's way of salvation always seems foolish (1 Cor. 1:20-21).

'The fear of the LORD is the beginning of wisdom' (Ps. 111:10). This is the kind of wisdom that opens the mind to understand the gospel, as it is revealed in the Bible. It is also the key to spiritual progress. Such wisdom comes from above and is born in your heart by the Holy Spirit. He is the one who opens the mind to understand the Scriptures. Failure to recognise this is the ruin of millions.

*'The LORD knows the thoughts of man;*
*he knows that they are futile'*
*(Ps. 94:11)*

࿇

## Ask for a Teachable Spirit

*'Teach me your way, O* LORD'
*(Ps. 27:11)*

'When ignorance is bliss, 'tis folly to be wise.' So runs the old proverb. In some circumstances, it is good advice, but where there is ignorance of the gospel it couldn't be worse. Many people are happy in their ignorance because they do not know their dreadful destiny. They are living in a fool's paradise.

Like true wisdom, true happiness is based on knowledge of the truth, and is grounded on a sure hope of a future inheritance. Writing to Christian believers who had never seen Jesus, the apostle Peter says: 'Though you have not seen him, you love him; and even though you do not see him now, you believe in him and are filled with an inexpressible and glorious joy, for you are receiving the goal of your faith, the salvation of your souls' (1 Peter 1:8-9).

The words of Zophar, one of Job's would-be comforters were not very helpful, but at least, he got this right: 'The joy of the godless lasts but a moment. Though his pride reaches to the heavens and his head touches the clouds, he will perish for ever...' (Job 20:5-7). By contrast, true happiness, being based on the knowledge of the everlasting truth, lasts for ever.

If God has blessed you with a desire to know him, he will give you a teachable spirit. You must set aside your preconceived ideas. In particular, you must abandon the notion, usually cherished by unbelievers, that you are the master of your own destiny. As you read God's word, you will soon discover that eternal life is his gift. You cannot earn it and you do not deserve it. 'For the wages of sin is death, but the gift of God is eternal life in Christ Jesus our Lord' (Rom. 6:23).

Our desperate need for knowledge of God tends to be forgotten these days. The idea is abroad that having a warm heart is better than having an informed mind — as if the two were opposites. But a warm heart soon grows cold if it is not constantly fed with knowledge. It is possible, of course, to stuff your head with knowledge that never reaches the heart. The sooner you realise, however, that a truly joyful heart and an informed mind belong together, the better it will be for you. Indeed, in the New Testament the words 'heart' and 'mind' mean virtually the same thing.

The words of the psalmist express this vital truth. Notice carefully how he speaks of the relationship between his heart-experience and his knowledge of God's word: 'I have hidden your word in my heart that I might not sin against you. Praise be to you, O LORD; teach me your decrees … I rejoice in following your statutes as one rejoices in great riches' (Ps. 119:11,12,14). Such rejoicing never fades. Indeed, it gets better the more you learn what God has done, and will yet do for you.

A teachable spirit therefore is crucial for your spiritual development. In particular, it is essential for your growth in confidence that God's word is trustworthy. With this gift, the day will come, if it has not dawned already, when you will re-joice that your name is written in heaven (Luke 10:20). If it has dawned, your rejoicing can only increase along with your assurance and your knowledge of the Scriptures.

You are already persuaded of God's existence. You must now go a step further and believe that he 'richly blesses all who call on him' (Rom.10:12). A mere belief in his existence is of little value. Millions believe it, and perish. The New Testament puts it like this: 'And without faith it is impossible to please God, because anyone who comes to him must believe that he exists and that he rewards those who earnestly seek him' (Heb. 11:6). To this subject we now turn.

*'Who, then, is the man that fears the LORD?*
*He will instruct him in the way chosen for him'*
*(Ps. 25:12)*

৵

## Face the Truth

*'All have sinned and fall short of the glory of God'*
*(Rom. 3:23)*

A thousand voices are clamouring for your attention. They are all shouting at once and every one of them is claiming to proclaim the truth. Many people give up their quest for truth because they cannot distinguish between the conflicting claims. But it is different for you. Since, by God's grace, you are now willing to hold to the teaching of Jesus, he has promised that 'you will know the truth, and the truth will set you free' (John 8:32). This is a great privilege.

To know the truth we need to turn to the Scriptures. There is no better way to find out how you stand before God. In spite of all the voices that are raised to the contrary, the Bible is God's word. Your attitude to it will determine your destiny. All who choose to ignore what God has to say, will die in their sins.

For all who want to find their way to heaven, the bad news must come first. The reason for this is that you will never appreciate the good news until you have thoroughly digested the bad. Because some people react in anger when they hear the bad news, many preachers think it wise to tone it down in order to avoid offence. They try to persuade their hearers to trust in the Lord Jesus, but say little or nothing about God's judgment on those who refuse to do so (2 Thess. 1:8-9).

Now why would anyone want to trust in Jesus if he does not know why he should? No doctor worth his salt would try to persuade his terminally ill patients to take the treatment they need without telling them why they need it. Why should they take the pills if they are not convinced of the doctor's diagnosis?

Of course, we do not like being told that our sins are deeply offensive to God, and that unless something is done about them, we shall perish eternally. God's verdict however is clear: 'There is no-one righteous, not even one; there is no-one who understands, no-one who seeks God. All have turned away, they have together become worthless; there is no-one who does good, not even one' (Rom. 3:10-12).

It is futile to argue with this, 'for whatever the law says, it says to all who are under the law, so that every mouth may be silenced and the whole world held accountable to God. Therefore no-one will be declared righteous in his sight by observing the law; rather, through the law we become conscious of sin' (Rom. 3:19-20). God's commandments cannot save us. All they can do is to reveal to us the extent to which we have fallen short of them.

The Bible is not saying that we are all necessarily guilty of robbery, violence, adultery or murder, but that we have all fallen short of the standard God has set, some in one way, some in another (Rom. 3:23). Our problem stems from what we are, because what we do is the outcome of what we are. So that, by nature, not one of us is acceptable to him. We are under God's condemnation and deserve nothing but eternal separation from him (John 3:18).

Now this is a very hard pill to swallow. Countless numbers of people have been lost eternally because their pride would not allow them to take it. But take it you must. God is against those who refuse from the start because, as we saw earlier, he 'opposes the proud but gives grace to the humble' (James 4:6). 'If we claim we have not sinned, we make him (God) out to be a liar and his word has no place in our lives' (1 John 1:10).

Much more could be said, but this is the substance of the first step. If you are not yet persuaded that, by nature, you are under condemnation, do not go to the Second Step until you are. No one ever rejoices in the forgiveness of sins and the assurance of eternal life, unless they have willingly taken this first step. No-one who refuses to humble himself before God and to face up to the truth about himself will be blessed with the high privileges enjoyed by true believers.

*'Your iniquities have separated you from your God...'*
*(Isa. 59:2)*

# STEP 2:
# BELIEVE IN GOD

*'The fool says in his heart, "There is no God"'*
*(Ps. 14:1)*

What I have said so far is based on the assumption that you believe in God. Nothing is more foolish than to deny his existence. But we need to look more closely into what it means to believe in God. By wilfully rejecting the evidence of his own eyes, the atheist puts himself on the same level as animals who cannot know God.

But who is the God we believe in? Most importantly, he is revealed as three Persons in one God — Father, Son and Holy Spirit. He is sovereign over his creation, which means that he orders and controls everything. He is infinite. His will is absolute. Everything he is and does is perfect. He gives himself in love to those whom he chooses, saving them from the appalling consequences of their sins and bringing them safely to heaven.

Now if you have sustained the assault on your pride in Step 1 and are still eager to go further, you have cause to thank God. As we proceed, still keep in mind that all you need to know is revealed in the Bible and nowhere else, because 'all Scripture is God breathed' (2 Tim. 3:16).

*'Without faith it is impossible to please God,*
*because anyone who comes to him must believe*

*that he exists and that he rewards*
*those who earnestly seek him'*
*(Heb. 11:6)*

&

## God in Three Persons

*'Therefore go and make disciples of all nations,*
*baptising them in the name of the Father*
*and of the Son and of the Holy Spirit.'*
*(Matt. 28:19)*

The French poet Voltaire (1694-1778) was being cynical when
he said that if God did not exist it would be necessary to invent
him. But even though he does exist, many people still find it
necessary to invent him. The necessity is widely felt because
of a natural hostility towards God as he is revealed in the Bible
(Rom. 8:7). But what sort of a God do they invent instead? The
list is almost endless. He may be an impersonal force of some
kind, or a bearded old man like Father Christmas. He may be a
God similar in some ways to the God of the Bible except that
permissiveness has replaced his justice and tolerance his wrath.

Like the word 'God', the word 'believe' is also capable of
serious misunderstanding. It may mean anything from merely
accepting the existence of something to absolute trust in a person. If I say 'I believe in ghosts', I do not mean that I trust in
them. But if I say 'I believe in my wife', it means that I trust
her implicitly. When someone says 'I believe in God', however,
it is impossible to know what he means. Does he merely believe in God's existence, or does he trust in him? According to
the apostle James, even demons believe in God's existence, and
shudder (James 2:19).

Make a habit of checking what others say about God
against his word, the Bible. You may find this hard at first, but

you will quickly improve your skill. The same habit must also apply to your own preconceived ideas. Check them against the Scriptures as well. Always remember that learning *about* God is necessary but not life changing of itself. Obviously, in any friendship, we need some knowledge of the other person before the relationship can develop. The same is true of God. If you have a desire to know him, you must first know about him.

Among the first things you should know about God is that he is a Person. You cannot have a relationship with an impersonal force. God is also a righteous Person who demands your repentance (Acts 17:30). He is a trustworthy Person with whom you may enjoy a personal and loving relationship. He is a gracious Person, from whom you may receive pardon. He is a just Person who will not allow you to be happy with sin.

What is revealed in Scripture about God will raise many unanswerable questions in your mind. This is because we are finite and God is infinite, This is where that teachable spirit we talked about earlier comes in. If you now have this precious gift from God, you will not reject truth just because you cannot get your mind round it. If we take it far enough, everything about God is beyond our understanding. But now that the door has opened for you, go through it, without doubting. This is the only way to make progress.

Who can get his mind round the Trinity — three Persons in one God? Yet, it is basic to the Christian faith. Many people have tried to illustrate the Trinity. Some have pointed to the threefold make-up of man, some to a three-leaf clover, and others to three-dimensional space and so on, but the attempt is vain. Human logic serves no purpose here. No one can understand how God can be three Persons in one God — God the Father, God the Son, and God the Holy Spirit — each Person being fully God. And no one ever makes progress in the Christian life unless he believes it.

If, however, you are now ready to rely on God's word, he will open your mind to understand a great deal *about* the Trinity.

You will discover for example, that each Person has a particular role. Before time began, the Father planned the creation of the universe and the redemption of his people. The Son created the universe and holds it together (Col. 1:16-17). In obedience to his Father's will, he accomplished redemption for us. He was stricken for the transgression of his people (Isa. 53:8). The Holy Spirit applies the benefits of Christ's redemption to all who believe, giving them new life and ensuring a safe entrance into the glory of heaven. He lives in their hearts, guides them into all truth and helps them to bring glory to his Name (John 16:13-14). The Father has elevated the Son to a supreme position. He is Lord of creation and Lord of the church. He is the first person to rise forever from the dead (Col. 1:18). He is now praying for his people (Heb. 7:25). He is coming again in glory to judge the world (Acts 10:42) and to gather his people together to be with him for ever (1 Thess. 4:17).

It is important for you to know that Christ's death and intercession belong together. As a faithful High Priest, he is interceding for you right now because he died for you. There is absolutely no danger that his prayers for you will not be answered. 'He is able to save completely those who come to God through him, because he always lives to intercede for them' (Heb. 7:25).

To whet your appetite for further study, here are three texts to think about. Speaking of God the Father and God the Son, Paul the apostle says: 'But when the time had fully come, God sent his Son, born of a woman, born under law, to redeem those under law' (Gal. 4:4). Speaking of God the Son, the same apostle says: 'For by him all things were created: things in heaven and on earth, visible and invisible, whether thrones or powers or rulers or authorities; all things were created by him and for him' (Col. 1:16). Speaking of all three Persons, the apostle Peter says that we '…have been chosen according to the foreknowledge of God the Father, through the sanctifying work of the Spirit, for obedience to Jesus Christ…' (1 Peter 1:2).

*'And now the Sovereign* LORD *has sent me, with his Spirit …*
*your Redeemer, the Holy One of Israel…'*
*(Isa. 48:16-17)*

৯

# God Is Sovereign

*'He does as he pleases with*
*the powers of heaven and the peoples of the earth.*
*No-one can hold back his hand or say to him:*
*"What have you done?"'*
*(Dan. 4:35)*

As a new believer, it may come as a surprise to know that Christians disagree about doctrine. Some give great importance to certain aspects of the truth that are relatively unimportant and behave as if nothing else mattered. Others, due to their ignorance of the Scriptures or loss of confidence in them, dispute over basic doctrines.

I mention this not only to warn you, but also because one of these important and basic doctrines, the Sovereignty of God, although clearly taught in Scripture, is now in dispute. Voices have been raised against it for centuries, but they are particularly strident at present. You may not yet realise the importance of this in the life of a believer, but for reasons I will mention later, the sooner you are convinced that God is in absolute control, the better.

This situation comes about because believers do sometimes find it hard to accept revealed truths that appear contrary to human logic. This is unbelief. The objectors usually work on the principle that *we* determine our destiny. If this were not so, they say, fatalism would be the only alternative. (Fatalism is the belief that everything that happens is unavoidable, so there is no point in trying to do anything about it.) But there is all the difference in the world between Divine Sovereignty and fatalism. Fatalists believe there is no God and everything that happens is without purpose. Like driftwood on a flooded river, we are all helpless and going nowhere in particular. God's sovereignty, on the other hand, means that he works out everything according to his purpose.

Others believe a second alternative. They say, 'If God predetermines everything that happens, human beings cannot be free. But since they *are* free, it follows that God cannot predetermine anything.' In other words, he is not sovereign. 'Is it not obvious', they ask, 'that the free actions of human beings have altered the course of history?' How then can God plan the future? To cope with an ever-changing situation, they believe that he is forced to keep changing his mind.

Some of these objectors are eager to remind us that the Bible speaks of God changing his mind. For example, as early as Genesis chapter six we read that 'The LORD was grieved that he had made man on the earth, and his heart was filled with pain. So the LORD said, "I will wipe mankind, whom I have created, off from the face of the earth — men and animals, and creatures that move along the ground, and birds of the air — for I am grieved that I have made them"' (Gen. 6:6-7). On the face of it, it seems that the wickedness of men took God by surprise so that he had to change his mind.

This form of writing, however, is a concession to our ignorance. Language that we readily understand is being used to convey how God feels about human sin. It cannot be otherwise because since God is all-powerful, all knowing and outside of time altogether, human behaviour cannot take him by surprise. How can he be God if he is unable to work out everything 'in conformity with the purpose of his will' (Eph. 1:11)? To be confident that before the world was made, God planned to redeem his people from the appalling consequences of their sins and bring them safely to glory is one of the joys of the Christian life (Titus 1:2).

It must surely be obvious to you that if God *does* change his mind and his purposes are thwarted by the whims of men, there can be no security for any of us. For if he can make a blunder, how can he protect his children from being tested beyond their strength (1 Cor. 10:13)? You will save yourself a lot of needless anxiety if you are persuaded at an early stage in your Christian life that no circumstance can arise that will prevent God from achieving everything he has planned and promised.

Jesus sums it up in a single sentence. Speaking of those he came to save, he says: 'I give them eternal life, and they shall never perish; no-one can snatch them out of my hand.' Then he adds: 'My Father, who has given them to me, is greater than all; no-one can snatch them out of my Father's hand' (John 10:28-29). Along with many of God's promises, this simply cannot be true if God is unable to accomplish his will.

Therefore, do not let doubters or false teachers influence you. They are trying to rob God of his glory and you of your joy. As with God the Holy Trinity, so it is with God's sovereignty — both are beyond our understanding. How God accomplishes his will in this turbulent world and still holds men responsible for their actions is a mystery. But the Bible teaches both very clearly.

If then, you rely on the Bible, even if you cannot fathom its teaching, you will be able to rejoice daily in the fact that God chose you in Christ before the creation of the world (Eph. 1:4), and will watch over you until you reach the glory of heaven (1 Peter 1:5). At the same time, you will not feel free to do as you please, but rather you will have a desire to live to please God as a responsible human being.

Of course, there are some things God cannot do. He cannot lie, he cannot die, and he cannot be faithless. But this merely confirms his trustworthiness to do exactly what he has promised.

*'Ah, Sovereign* LORD, *you have made the heavens and the earth*
*by your great power and outstretched arm.*
*Nothing is too hard for you'*
*(Jer. 32:17)*

৵

## God Is Holy

*'Be holy because I, the* LORD *your God, am holy'*
*(Lev. 19:2)*

A member of the church in which I once served, would not set foot in the chancel — the area of the church interior where the choir usually sits — because, he regarded it as holy. In his view, places are made holy by being consecrated by men. Once so consecrated, he believed, they are out of bounds to common people like himself.

Holiness however has primarily to do with character. Where human beings are concerned, it is God-likeness in the market place. In this sense, God calls every believer to be holy. Like a diamond cutter, he takes the rough diamond and, using the rough and tumble of life, he removes all the sharp corners and unwanted bits. His ultimate purpose is to cut and polish our lives so that every facet combines to reflect the glory of God, Jesus himself being our pattern. 'For those God foreknew he also predestined to be conformed to the likeness of his Son…' (Rom. 8:29). The process begins right now.

Therefore, since being holy is being like Jesus, the importance of reading the Scriptures to discover what Jesus is like is obvious. He is the perfect representation of God, so that if we want to know what God is like, it is to Jesus that we must look. For 'the Son is the radiance of God's glory and the exact representation of his being' (Heb. 1:3).

Like Father, like Son! The revelation of God's glory and majesty revealed in the moral excellence and matchless purity of Jesus is sufficient for all our need. Just as God the Father is holy in nature, and separate from everything evil, so is God the Son. And since everything God the Father does is perfect, so everything God the Son does is perfect. His deeds are perfect. His love is perfect. His justice is perfect.

Paul describes God the Father as 'the blessed and only Ruler, the King of kings and Lord of lords, who alone is immortal and who lives in unapproachable light, whom no-one has seen or can see' (1 Tim. 6:15-16). As the apostle John explains, it is the Son who makes the Father known: 'No-one has ever seen God, but God the One and Only, who is at the Father's side, has made him known' (John 1:18).

You should make it your duty to develop a keen awareness of God's holiness, both its positive and negative aspects. This will help you to see yourself as you really are. Since sin is sin because God is holy, there is no better way. With this awareness, you will experience a freedom not known before — a freedom to live for God in this world. This is certainly something you could never do formerly.

Before your conversion, you probably insisted, as many do, that you had never done this or that, as if holiness were entirely negative. This will now be anathema to you. Instead, you will focus on how God wants you to live. You will discover that holiness is very positive. (We shall look at the gravity of sin in Step 4.)

Nevertheless, you should not forget that many of God's commandments *are* negative, beginning with the words 'you shall not'. But the essence of holiness is mainly positive. It is about loving God and others. Jesus made this clear in his summary of the law: '"Love the Lord your God with all your heart and with all your soul and with all your mind." This is the first and greatest commandment. And the second is like it: "Love your neighbour as yourself"' (Matt. 22:37-39). There's nothing negative about that!

An awareness of God's holiness will also help you to live that humble life we talked about in Step 1. It will enable you to live in the fear of God. It will encourage you to be reverent in worship. It will help you to face up to the seriousness of your sins and to grieve over them. 'God's kindness leads you towards repentance' (Rom. 2:4).

The Bible furnishes us with several accounts of people who were content with themselves until they came face to face with the glory of God. Job tells us that he had heard about the Lord God, but when he was brought face to face with him, he cried out, 'I despise myself and repent in dust and ashes' (Job 42:5-6). When the prophet Isaiah 'saw the Lord,' he too cried out: 'Woe to me! … I am a man of unclean lips, and I live among a people of unclean lips, and my eyes have seen the King, the LORD Almighty' (Isa 6:5). Isaiah's reaction reminds me of my own experience when I first 'saw' the Lord. Almost immediately, I became deeply ashamed of my foul mouth.

When Peter, a disciple of Jesus, saw his power and glory in a miraculous catch of fishes, he fell down on his knees and said: 'Go away from me, Lord; I am a sinful man!' (Luke 5:8). His deep conviction of sin blotted out the emergency that had arisen with the overloaded fishing boats.

*Who may ascend the hill of the LORD?*
*Who may stand in his holy place?*
*He who has clean hands and a pure heart,*
*who does not lift up his soul to an idol*
*or swear by what is false.*
*He will receive blessing from the LORD'*
*(Ps. 24:3-5)*

෨

## God Is Love

*'For God so loved the world that*
*he gave his one and only Son,*
*that whoever believes in him shall not perish*
*but have eternal life'*
*(John 3:16)*

Because so much sentimental nonsense is circulating about God's love, you would be well advised to search the Scriptures to discover the truth for yourself. Listening only to what others say, even if they are believers, is not always a safe option these days because many have a very vague or unbalanced view of divine love.

One will tell you that God loves you, but without saying anything about his wrath or his demand for repentance. This sentimentalises his love and robs him of his justice. Another will go a little further and say God loves you so much that Christ died for you, but will not say why he had to die. This robs the gospel of meaning. Yet another will try to persuade you that if you want to experience God's love, you must take the initiative because God will never do anything unless you make the first move. This robs him of his sovereignty.

To avoid living with uncertainty you must recognise the inadequacy of these opinions. As I said just now, be determined to inform your mind about God's love from the Scriptures. If you do, you will not go astray. You will understand that once you are born of the Spirit, nothing can separate you from the love of God that is in Christ Jesus our Lord (Rom. 8:38-39).

You will also discover that God's loving protection of his people cannot fail because he has the power to prevail over every contrary influence. Gradually, your assurance that God 'is able to keep you from falling and to present you before his glorious presence without fault and with great joy' (Jude 24), will increase. Being free from uncertainty you will be able to enjoy God, as you should.

Without doubt, John 3:16 (quoted at the beginning of this section) is the best-known verse in the Bible. It is also one of the most misunderstood. It is frequently taken to mean that God's redeeming love is freely available to all but he does not actively seek a relationship with anyone. That is to say, his love is passive. If this were true, it would mean that Christ died without having anyone particular in mind. If you picture God as a loving father waiting hopefully but helplessly for his wandering children to come home, you will get the idea.

The notion is not only seriously mistaken, it is also a grave affront to Almighty God. In addition, it is bound to undermine the believer's confidence, making him feel that everything depends on him. That such an idea should have gained credence in the church exposes our ignorance of the Scriptures.

So, let it sink down into your heart from the beginning of your Christian life that you chose Christ because he chose you first. 'For he chose us in him before the creation of the world to be holy and blameless in his sight' (Eph. 1:4). And all the help you will need to remain faithful to him comes from above. It is God's gift to you. You belong to Christ because he drew you to himself — just as he did every other member of his family 'from every nation, tribe, people and language' (Rev. 7:9).

But God's love extends even further. Listen again to Paul's words: 'If God is for us, who can be against us? He who did not spare his own Son, but gave him up for us all — how will he not also, along with him, graciously give us all things?' (Rom. 8:31-32). Jesus is God's greatest gift. Therefore, he is the guarantee of every other good and perfect gift. What does this include? It includes everything you need from the time you were born anew, right through to the time when you will receive your resurrection body — a body no longer subject to sickness, decay or death. It includes the perfect joy of heaven in God's presence for ever.

*'We love because he first loved us'*
*(1 John 4:19)*
☙

## God Is Trustworthy

*'Great is your faithfulness'*
*(Lam. 3:23)*

I was on holiday with my wife and children. Walking along the beach late one afternoon, we bumped into an old friend who had just been water skiing. He noticed my two teenagers' eyes light up and asked them if they would like to learn. You can guess the answer. We arranged to meet the following morning for a training session. My children were so excited they had difficulty in getting to sleep. The next morning we arrived before the arranged time, and we waited and waited … and waited, but our friend did not turn up. The speedboat was nowhere in sight. I was not at all pleased because our two trusting children were bitterly disappointed.

My grandma used to say: 'If you promise a child anything, whether it be a sweet or a smack, make sure you keep your promise.' But such wisdom is not common these days. How different it is with God. There is no possibility of disappointment where his promises are concerned. He will always remain faithful to his word, for he cannot deny himself (2 Tim. 2:13). No circumstances can ever arise in which he cannot be faithful. If you believe this, you will trust him implicitly.

In passing, notice how I have used the words 'believe' and 'trust' in the last sentence. As we saw earlier, the word 'believe' can mean nothing more than accepting the existence of something. The word 'trust' removes the ambiguity. There is a vast difference between *believing* that God exists and actually putting your *trust* in him.

When I was a child, I was taught that on the Day of Judgment, God would separate human beings into two groups — those who believe in God and those who don't. Those who believe would go to heaven and those who don't would go to hell. As far as I can remember, my tutors never explained what they meant by the word 'believe'. I was in danger of thinking that as long as I believed in God's existence, I would be safe. How much better it would have been if they had drawn the line between those who *trust* in God and those who don't.

I remember the time when the bond between the girl who is now my wife and me had not been established. I was keenly aware of her existence and I believed she was a trustworthy and honourable woman. But I had not had an opportunity to prove it. But later, when I put my trust in her and she in me, a loving and lasting relationship began. Now, her trustworthiness is no longer a matter of belief but of fact. How different it would have been if her trustworthiness had remained a piece of information in my head!

So it is with God. Believing truth *about* him changes nothing. Having a trustful relationship with him changes everything. The Scriptures tell us that Abraham 'did not waver through unbelief regarding the promise of God, but was strengthened in his faith and gave glory to God, being fully persuaded that God had power to do what he had promised' (Rom. 4:20-21). This means that Abraham trusted God's promise implicitly. Because of this — and this is important — God accepted sinful Abraham as if he were a righteous man. His faith was credited to him as righteousness.

Paul tells us that all who trust in Christ are Abraham's children! At first sight, this seems rather strange. But Abraham is our father in the sense that we have the same trust in God's promises as he did, and because of this, we too are accepted as righteous in God's sight (Gal. 3:29). To be sure, only those who trust God in this way are acceptable to him (See Step 5, Justification By Faith). Faith, for the Christian, is personal trust in a trustworthy God.

Trust is not a static thing however. Over the past fifty years, as my wife and I came to know each other better, my trust in her increased day by day. In the same way, as we get to know God better, our trust in him increases and — I say it again — so does our assurance of future glory. You must therefore, 'trust in the LORD with all your heart and lean not on your own understanding' (Prov. 3:5). You cannot trust the Lord *and* depend on your own understanding. It is either one or the other.

You will find, as I certainly have, that depending entirely on your own understanding does nothing to promote your spiritual well-being. For example, when facing temptation, I have always found that my own reasoning is very efficient at finding grounds for giving way to it. I have known believers — even believers of long standing — to use all kinds of warped arguments to justify their sin. If, at times of testing, we fail to trust in God's word, grievous sin is likely to be the outcome.

To be convinced that God is all-powerful and trustworthy will transform your life. Anxiety about your eternal destiny will no longer trouble you, and you will never have cause to be ashamed. Paul was suffering in a miserable Roman prison when he penned these triumphant words: 'Yet I am not ashamed, because I know whom I have believed, and am convinced that he is able to guard what I have entrusted to him' (2 Tim. 1:12).

In Step 3 we shall learn more about this important duty of trusting in God's word.

*'Blessed is the man who trusts in the LORD,*
*whose confidence is in him'*
*(Jer. 17:7)*

# STEP 3:
# TRUST GOD'S WORD

*'Scripture cannot be broken'*
*(John 10:35)*

Apart from creation, the Scriptures are the only authentic source of the knowledge of God. And they reveal much more about him than his creation does. We now briefly consider why it is reasonable to trust them. To submit to any kind of authority is unpopular today, and the authority of the Bible is no exception. Nevertheless, if you are to make progress in your new life, confidence in the authority of the Bible is vital.

In any other science you would put yourself above your subject. To gain knowledge of God however, you must place yourself under your subject. With that God-given teachable spirit we talked about earlier, you will be able to overcome popular scepticism about the reliability of God's word. You will discover that submission to Scripture sets you free.

You will also discover that such submission is character-forming. As you focus on God's word, 'wisdom will enter your heart, and knowledge will be pleasant to your soul' (Prov. 2:10). The reason is simple. 'The LORD gives wisdom, and from his mouth come knowledge and understanding' (Prov. 2:6).

The reading of Scripture involves both mind and heart. Do not be influenced by those for whom ecstatic feeling is more important than the day-to-day outworking of the knowledge of God.

## God's Word Is Trustworthy

*'All his precepts are trustworthy'*
*(Ps. 111:7)*

When long distances separated me from my future wife, we wrote love letters to each other. In her absence, they meant a lot to me. Now I was certainly not in love with the letters, even though they were written in the finest handwriting on high quality paper with a hint of perfume. Not at all. The letters were valuable because I was in love with the writer.

So it is with the Bible. We treasure it, not because it is a family heirloom or because it may be written on fine India paper and bound in leather. Over the years, I have thrown many Bibles away because they were falling to bits. The one I am using at present is written on cheap paper and is going the same way as the rest. No, we love the Bible because it is the word of the God we love. Why did the Psalmist say: 'I delight in your commands because I love them' (Ps. 119:47)? It was because he loved the Lord whose commands they were.

The old proverb — 'love me love my dog' — makes the point that if we really love someone, we shall also love what is his, including his dog. In some cases this may not be easy, especially if he has a Rottweiler with sharp teeth, or a bulldog that slavers all over your best suit. But it is certainly true in this case. For if we love God, we shall love what is his. No one makes progress in the Christian life unless he realises that loving God and loving his word belong together. To love God is to love his word.

If, therefore, you love God and put your trust in him because you believe he is trustworthy, you will love and trust his word because you believe that too is trustworthy. What sense would it make to say: 'I trust my wife but I don't believe what she says'? Besides, without the Scriptures, we would have no way of knowing that God is trustworthy, and a loving relationship with him would be impossible.

In spite of this, many people, including some who are supposed to be church leaders, refuse to submit to the authority
of the Bible. They may make a pretence of doing so, but closer
enquiry reveals their reservations. They justify their position in
the church with great skill, but are in fact blind leaders of the
blind and do a lot of damage (Matt. 15:14). There is nothing
new in this. Sceptic scholars have been trying to demolish the
reliability of the Bible for very many years. It is Satan's old trick,
'Did God really say...?' (Gen. 3:1).

Confidence in Scripture has been further eroded by the
widespread rejection of all forms of authority in our society.
Being told what to do and what not to do goes against the
grain. Prohibitions like 'You shall not commit adultery' (Exod.
20:14) are regarded as an assault on our freedom. But it is those
who refuse to submit whose freedom is curtailed. As we saw
earlier, they are free, as Paul puts it, 'from the control of righteousness' but that is because they are 'slaves to sin' which results in death (Rom. 6:20).

If you really want to grow stronger in your newly found
faith, you must rise above these shameful trends and take God's
word to heart as it stands. One of the most convincing reasons
why you should do this is that Jesus did it. 'I tell you the truth,'
he said, 'until heaven and earth disappear, not the smallest letter, not the least stroke of a pen, will by any means disappear
from the Law until everything is accomplished' (Matt. 5:18).

There is always the problem of accurate translation of
course, and it is useful to have different versions to hand. These
days, if the translators are not sure what the Hebrew or Greek
means, they offer an alternative version. For English readers,
every help is to hand.

The apostles followed Jesus in this matter. Peter is very clear:
'Above all, you must understand that no prophecy of Scripture
came about by the prophet's own interpretation. For prophecy
never had its origin in the will of man, but men spoke from God
as they were carried along by the Holy Spirit' (2 Peter 1:20-21).

The apostles were emphatic about the divine authority of their own writings too. They are now part of Holy Scripture. Paul writes to the Thessalonians: 'And we also thank God continually because, when you received the word of God, which you heard from us, you accepted it not as the word of men, but as it actually is, the word of God, which is at work in you who believe' (1 Thess. 2:13).

The ability of human beings to communicate with each other is marvellous. But it is not surprising. Since God is a God who speaks and we are made in his image, it is only to be expected that we too have this astonishing gift (Gen. 1:26). The revelation of God in creation leaves those who refuse to acknowledge him without excuse (Rom. 1:20). People who have a greater knowledge of the Scriptures will also suffer greater punishment if they wilfully violate them.

Some would say there is a third way to know God because God is supremely revealed in the Person of Jesus Christ. This is true, but it is not really a third way because we are entirely dependent on the Scriptures for our knowledge of Christ.

Finally, like all three of my children, you may have been taught in school that evolution over millions of years is a proven fact and this may have undermined your confidence in the Scriptures. Do not believe it. In spite of the many institutions that hold on obstinately to Darwin's theory (usually because they do not like the alternatives), they have been largely discounted. Neo-Darwinism is going the same way. The so-called missing link from apes to men has never been found, and every attempt to build an ape-man from a few bones has ended in failure.

The law of entropy (disorder) is a fatal blow to the idea of evolution. If left to itself, everything that is organised and/or beautiful would become disorganised and ugly. And if there is any life left in the sacred cow of atheistic evolution, the science of genetics will finish it off. In any case, the theory of evolution is just that — a theory. Since it is constantly changing as new discoveries are made, it is not a safe place to look for eternal truth.

Now since the subject of God speaking is of great interest to many Christians today — and a source of much confusion — it is important for you to understand what the Bible teaches on the subject. To this we now turn.

*'You are in error because you do not*
*know the Scriptures or the power of God'*
*(Matt. 22:29)*

ȷ

## God Speaks

*'In the past God spoke to our forefathers through the prophets*
*at many times and in various ways,*
*but in these last days he has spoken to us by his Son'*
*(Heb. 1:1-2)*

Imagine trying to establish a friendship with someone if you did not have the ability to communicate! Everyone knows that human relationships depend on communication in one form or another. Between believers, it is a means of joyful fellowship. What is not commonly realised however is that it is also a means of fellowship between man and his Maker. Indeed, God created us for this purpose.

Imagine too, what a mess we would be in if God never communicated with us. Thankfully, it is not so. The Bible begins with God speaking and, as is frequently the case, his words are followed by his actions: 'And God said, "Let there be light," and there was light' (Gen. 1:3).

The Old Testament provides many examples of God speaking through the prophets. We saw in the last section that prophecy never had its origin in the will of man, but holy men spoke from God as they were carried along by the Holy Spirit (2 Peter 1:21). The Lord Jesus himself is described as the Word of God (John 1:1), because he is the one who reveals God's truth. Of course, there were long periods when God was silent during the two thousand years or so in which the Scriptures were written.

You should understand that God does not speak directly to men today, audibly or otherwise, in a way that adds to his revelation in the Bible. I mention this because you will almost certainly encounter people who attach more importance to seeing visions and hearing voices than they do to the written word. All too often, the messages they claim to receive run contrary to the teaching of Scripture, so that verification is impossible. I have known people who tried to justify foolish and even immoral actions on this basis.

Of course, you may be persuaded at some time in the future, that a certain course of action is in line with God's will — like moving house, changing jobs, or getting married — but this is a different matter altogether. In these circumstances, you should thoroughly test your conviction against the general principles of Christian behaviour laid down in the Scriptures and by consultation with other more mature believers.

Further revelations are unnecessary because the Bible is sufficient. The writer to the Hebrews tells us that in Old Testament days, 'God spoke to our forefathers through the prophets at many times and in various ways, but in these last days he has spoken to us by his Son' (Heb. 1:1-2). The message of the prophets in the Old Testament, although an essential preparation for the coming of Christ, was incomplete. Now that God has spoken by his Son, there is nothing more to be said.

Nevertheless, God does still speak. What he says however is not new, but a powerful restating of timeless truths already revealed. That is to say, he speaks through his creation and through his word to people who are alive, just as he did in the past to people who are long since dead. Through his creation, he still reveals his 'invisible qualities — his eternal power and divine nature' so that men who do not acknowledge him are without excuse (Rom. 1:20). Through his word, he reveals Christ to each generation as the only way of salvation for lost sinners.

Do remember then that to find your way to heaven, you will find all the information you need in the pages of Holy Scripture. You must take to heart what it says, and not what you would like it to say.

*'See to it that you do not refuse him who speaks'*
*(Heb. 12:25)*

≈

## Think!

*'Do not conform any longer to the pattern of this world,*
*but be transformed by the renewing of your mind.*
*Then you will be able to test and approve what God's will is —*
*his good, pleasing and perfect will'*
*(Rom. 12:2)*

Some religious people give the impression that the Christian answer to human wisdom is mindless emotionalism. They work on the bizarre principle that the Holy Spirit relieves them of the responsibility of using their brains. You should always be on your guard against these people. Having swallowed the lie that the use of the mind is a hindrance to progress, they never make any.

Inevitably, when feeling becomes more important than thinking, spiritual growth comes to a standstill. People of this type may appear, at times, to be full of joy but it is shallow and short-lived. The promises of God, by contrast, thrill the heart as they take root in the believing mind.

The Scriptures do not encourage mindless enthusiasm. Since God is an intelligent Being (Isa. 1:18) and we are made in his likeness (Gen. 1:26), we too are intelligent beings. To switch our brains off is to deny our humanity. Again, we have the example of Jesus. He encouraged his disciples to use their minds. He told them to look at the birds and the flowers, and think! (Matt. 6:26,28). He challenged his opponents by quoting words from the Old Testament and telling them to go and learn their meaning (Matt. 9:13). Frequently he left his hearers to work out the meaning of his parables.

Paul too prayed earnestly that God would fill the minds of believers with the knowledge of God's will through all spiritual wisdom and understanding (Col. 1:9). The apostle is asking God to make good all the gaps in their knowledge of God. Of course, these gaps are not filled without the help of the Holy Spirit, but neither are they filled if we refuse to think.

Now please follow me carefully — as the Spirit transforms your heart, he transforms your mind as well — never the one without the other. As we saw in Step 2, the New Testament uses both 'mind' and 'heart' to refer to our inner being. When Paul speaks about being 'transformed by the renewing of your mind' (Rom. 12:2), he is talking about a change in the whole person.

So then, if you are to understand the glory of the gospel and your personal interest in it, you must stretch your mind to comprehend as much as you can of revealed truth. You must read, and think about what you read. You must turn it over and over in your mind. As you do so, you will discover that the Scriptures liberate and sharpen your mind as nothing else can.

After all, this is what Godly wisdom is all about. Deepening convictions in your heart/mind will play a vital and increasing role in your daily life. On this basis, even if you live to be a hundred years old, God's word will still be exercising your mind, changing your heart and delighting your soul.

The Book of Proverbs says: 'My son, if you accept my words and store up my commands within you, turning your ear to wisdom and applying your heart to understanding, and if you call out for insight and cry aloud for understanding, and if you look for it as for silver and search for it as for hidden treasure, then you will understand the fear of the LORD and find the knowledge of God' (Prov. 2:1 5). Nowhere will you find better advice.

'We speak of God's secret wisdom,' says Paul, 'a wisdom that has been hidden and that God destined for our glory before time began' (1 Cor. 2:7). The word 'wisdom' here stands for God's revealed truth in the gospel. And the word 'glory' embraces all the glorious blessings that Christ has secured for us through the gospel. The apostle is still thinking of these blessings as he continues: "'No eye has seen, no ear has heard, no mind has conceived what God has prepared for those who love him" — but God has revealed it to us by his Spirit' (1 Cor. 2:9-10).

Who could possibly fail to see that all this involves the mind? With the enlightenment of the Spirit, increasing knowledge of revealed truth will enable you to comprehend more and more how privileged you are! And for this you must constantly give thanks to God. If he did not open your mind to understand the Scriptures (Luke 24:45), you would never acquire the ability to rejoice in your glorious destiny, not even if you lived a million years.

Those foolish people who do not think it worthwhile to retain the knowledge of God are in danger of being given over to a 'depraved mind' (Rom. 1:28). A 'depraved mind' is a mind so blinded that it cannot break out of the cycle of evil. A person with such a mind has ceased thinking straight and is no longer teachable. Darkness has enveloped his understanding because of his own stupidity. This is a judicial act. God says, in effect: 'You abandon me, and I will abandon you.'

Finally, as you reflect on God's word, you must never think of faith and reason as being opposites. It is said that where reason stops, faith goes on. But it is far more accurate to say that where faithful reason stops, reasoning faith goes on. Although the gospel is much wider than the scope of the mind, none of it is unreasonable.

*'Then you will know the truth, and the truth will set you free'*
*(John 8:32)*

# STEP 4:
# FACE THE BAD NEWS

*'All have sinned and fall short*
*of the glory of God'*
*(Rom. 3:23)*

As we saw in Step 2, an increasing awareness of the holiness of God is essential if we are to make a realistic assessment of ourselves. By nature, in common with all human beings, we stand guilty before God. The likeness of God in which we were made has been marred by sin so that fellowship with him is impossible. As the prophet Isaiah says: 'Your iniquities have separated you from your God' (Isa. 59:2).

We come back to this subject because of its importance. To make light of sin is, sadly, a common practice. When Christians are guilty of it, it is not only an affront to the grace of God in Christ, but also a very serious hindrance to progress. To put it positively, your understanding and appreciation of the gospel and your spiritual growth depend on a lifelong awareness of the gravity of sin.

The Day of Judgment is coming. Apart from Christ, there is no hope for anyone. For God 'has set a day when he will judge the world with justice by the man he has appointed' (Acts 17:31). That man is Jesus. The only alternative to repentance and faith in Jesus Christ is to perish eternally.

## All Have Sinned

*'I know that nothing good lives in me,*
*that is, in my sinful nature'*
*(Rom. 7:18)*

I understand that about a million people in the United Kingdom are suffering from diabetes but don't know it. Being ignorant of their condition, they do not seek treatment. Millions more are suffering from the much more serious disease of sin and they don't know it either. Consequently, they too do not seek the remedy.

In my case, as soon as diabetes was diagnosed, the doctors and nurses explained the disease, its cause and effect, in detail. Indeed, one nurse reacted strongly when I suggested that my condition was mild. She described the diabetics she had known who had lost both feet and had gone blind! Clearly, she was warning me of the dangers of apathy.

As we saw earlier, a good doctor will explain to his patient why he needs treatment. Unless the patient realises the true nature of his condition, he is not likely to be diligent in taking the medicine. If his condition were life threatening, he would be very careful not to miss a single dose.

In the same way, no preacher worth his salt would try to persuade his hearers to put their trust in Christ without telling them why they need him. Yet, many preachers today do exactly that. They know very well that the spiritual condition of their hearers is perilous, but they will not say so. On this basis, they invite people to 'take the medicine' anyway. 'Don't worry,' they say, 'God loves you and Jesus died for you.' The response, if any, will be just as meaningless as the invitation.

Why do they do this? There can only be one reason. They are aware that some people react in anger when faced with the bad news. To avoid offence therefore, sin and judgment are muted or omitted altogether. To mutilate the gospel message in this way makes it ineffective. Why should anyone seek refuge in Christ if he does not know his life is in danger?

In Step 2, we saw that in the light of God's holiness we are all defiled — guilty of failing to keep his commandments. Consequently, we cannot appeal to the commandments to save us. All they can do is expose our sins. As Paul explains: 'Now we know that whatever the law says, it says to those who are under the law, so that every mouth may be silenced and the whole world held accountable to God. Therefore no-one will be declared righteous in his sight by observing the law; rather, through the law we become conscious of sin' (Rom. 3:19-20).

The consciousness of sin, however, does not bring with it a desire to change unless the Holy Spirit is at work. Our sinful nature is such that we rebel against God's commandments for '... the sinful mind is hostile to God. It does not submit to God's law, nor can it do so. Those controlled by the sinful nature cannot please God' (Rom. 8:7-8). The apostle also tells us that he would not have known that covetousness was a sin if God's law had not forbidden it. But when he made the discovery, instead of keeping the commandment, his sinful nature responded by producing every kind of covetous desire (Rom. 7:7-8). If God forbids it, I want to do it even more.

In passing, I should point out the danger of flattering yourself on the basis that there are some commandments you think you may have kept. For example, you may not have murdered anyone. But, according to Jesus, hatred in the heart makes us guilty of murder. Again, you may not have committed adultery but Jesus says that illicit sexual desire is adultery. In any case, 'whoever keeps the whole law' says the apostle James, 'and yet stumbles at just one point is guilty of breaking all of it' (James 2:10). By nature, we are not capable of keeping God's law, and therefore we are not naturally acceptable to him. We are under his condemnation and deserve nothing but eternal separation from him (John 3:18).

Sin then, is not merely a character defect that needs treatment, but an inherited spirit of rebellion against God that deserves punishment. It shows itself in violations of his commandments — that is to say, in transgressing what is forbidden and falling short of what is demanded. Further, sin has so marred the image of God in which we were created, we are left dissatisfied and unfulfilled. Every attempt to fill the gaping hole in our lives caused by sin always ends in failure. Try as we may, pleasure and wealth do not fill it. Nor do status, marriage, money, world travel, or acclaim. Only God can fill it.

Many theories have been proposed for the origin of man's moral nature, but Scripture provides the only satisfactory explanation: 'God created man in his own image, in the image of God he created him; male and female he created them' (Gen. 1:27). Adam had a *moral* likeness to God, a personality, and the ability to reason. (The name 'Adam' means 'man' or 'mankind'.) Animals do not have these characteristics.

Theories also abound to account for sin. According to the popular theory of evolution, higher forms of life like you and me developed by chance from the lower forms over millions of years, so that we developed ethical standards from our animal ancestors! In spite of the absurdity of the idea, many find it attractive because it removes the concept of accountability.

Therefore, it is in your own interest to reject the popular notion that Adam did not exist and that we are all well developed apes. (Evolution from one species to another remains a very shaky and unproven theory.) There is no reason whatever for you to doubt the Genesis account. According to Paul, writing under the inspiration of the Holy Spirit of God, 'sin entered the world through one man, and death through sin, and in this way death came to all men, because all sinned...' (Rom. 5:12). To try to evade the implications of this by taking refuge in the godless speculation of anti-Christian scholars is extremely foolish.

You should understand from this passage (Rom. 5:12) that God's forgiveness does not only cover what you do, but what you are. As the children of Adam, we share his guilt. Therefore, it is not your sins that make you a sinner. No! You are already a sinner by birth and that is why you sin.

We shall see later that being a Christian means having a new nature. This new nature comes from God, but it does not entirely displace the old sinful nature — at least, not yet. To the end of your life on earth, you will still fall short of God's standard. But rejoice in this — Christ's death covers all your future sins as well. God will not permit your sinful nature to control you. (Rom. 6:14).

As you may expect, the idea of our inheriting a sinful nature from Adam is rejected in our western society. But the verdict of Scripture could hardly be clearer: 'Just as through the disobedience of the one man' (Adam) 'the many were made sinners, so also through the obedience of the one man' (Christ) 'the many will be made righteous' (Rom. 5:19).

The apostle Paul refers to the two categories as those who are 'in Adam' (unbelievers) and those who are 'in Christ' (believers). God reckons all who are in Adam as sinners by nature and under condemnation. Those who are 'in Christ' he reckons as righteous by faith and no longer under condemnation.

The other day I saw a child — probably about two years old — throwing a tantrum. He was shouting, screaming, and trying to hit his mother. When she tried to pick him up, he went limp so that she could not get a grip on him. Did his mother or father teach him to behave like this? If not, then who? Certainly not God. The fact is, children do not need to be taught how to be naughty. They, like you and me, inherit it from their parents. It is in the genes.

For this reason God commands all people everywhere to repent (Acts 17:30). The implications of this are much wider than most people realise. It means changing our minds before God about the way our life is going. It means confessing our sins to him in deep sorrow, not only at the beginning of our new life but right through to the end of it. It means being prepared to forgive those who sin against us. It means acknowledging that we are sinners by nature. It means making restitution where possible for the wrong we have done. Not least, it means we are now willing to trust in Jesus Christ for our salvation. Genuine repentance always leads to a transformation of character. It indicates a willingness to do what God wants.

As we saw, no one likes being told that his sins are deeply offensive to God. But the Scripture stands: 'There is no-one righteous, not even one; there is no-one who understands, no-one who seeks God. All have turned away, they have together become worthless; there is no-one who does good, not even one' (Rom. 3:10-12). This means that (apart from Jesus) no one has ever come up to the standard God has set.

*Surely I was sinful at birth,*
*sinful from the time my mother conceived me.*
*(Ps. 51:5)*
ᔑ

## The Wages of Sin

*'For the wages of sin is death'*
*(Rom 6:23)*

When I was twelve years old, I went skating on a frozen pond near the school I attended. A day or two earlier, the headmaster had solemnly warned the boys that anyone caught skating on the pond would be severely punished. Someone observed my act of defiance and passed the information to the head. When he called me into his study I knew I was in serious trouble. He gave me a stern lecture and six strokes of the cane to make sure I did not forget it. I did not go skating on the pond again.

In this world punishment for doing wrong is not inevitable. Many people commit crime and are never caught. Not so with God. He never misses a thing. Punishment follows sin as sure as night follows day, although perhaps not always so quickly. It may not even be in this life, but it will surely come. It is not vindictiveness or revenge on God's part but simply a matter of justice. Just as a worker deserves his wages, so the sinner deserves his just punishment for violating God's law (Rom 6:23).

The person who does not believe in Jesus Christ does not have to wait for the verdict. It has already been given. He 'stands condemned already because he has not believed in the name of God's one and only Son' (John 3:18). Unbelievers, therefore, live in this world in a state of spiritual death. In this condition, the wrath of God remains on them because they are 'by nature objects of wrath' (Eph 2:3).

Not one of us can escape what we might call the natural punishments for sin. If, for example, I am lazy, I will suffer deprivation. If I abuse my body by drinking to excess, my health will suffer. This is because of the way God has made us. There are also temporal divine punishments. If, as a Christian, I am unfaithful to my wife, I must not expect God to leave me in peace. Our main concern here, however, is the terrible nature of eternal punishment. The Bible does not go into too much detail but what it says is enough. It speaks of 'everlasting destruction', 'blackest darkness', 'shame and everlasting contempt' and 'everlasting ruin'.

Do not think for a moment that you have a natural capability to avoid such a terrible destiny. It would be easier for you to pick yourself up by your shoelaces than to repent without God's help. God's command to repent, like the rest of his commands, is not something you can naturally comply with. The ability to obey the command is God's gift, whereby your whole being is brought into subjection to his will.

We read in the Acts of the Apostles that God exalted Jesus 'to his own right hand as Prince and Saviour that he might give repentance and forgiveness of sins to Israel' (Acts 5:31). As for the Jews, so also for the Gentiles: 'So then, God has even granted the Gentiles repentance unto life' (Acts 11:18).

Of course, Christians do not repent just once. Throughout life, every sin must be followed quickly by repentance. It must become an attitude of life.

It will help you to keep in mind 'that God's kindness leads you towards repentance' (Rom 2:4). So, think deeply and often about the cross where Jesus died, 'the righteous for the unrighteous, to bring you to God' (1 Peter 3:18). Meditate on his love and mercy to you, a sinner. Contemplate his goodness in paying the penalty for your sin, and for providing full and free salvation to all who repent and believe the gospel. Remember the high price God paid so that you would be able to say, along with King David of Israel: 'Blessed is the man whose sin the Lord will never count against him' (Rom 4:8).

*But unless you repent,*
*you too will all perish'*
*(Luke 13:3)*
و

## Judgment

*But because of your stubbornness and your unrepentant heart,*
*you are storing up wrath against yourself*
*for the day of God's wrath,*
*when his righteous judgment will be revealed'*
*(Rom. 2:5)*

A little more must be said about judgment. The Bible tells us that one day, those who stubbornly refuse to repent and believe the gospel will find themselves standing before the Judge of all the earth. A book will be opened before him in which the names of all those whom Christ honours are written (Phil. 4:3; Rev. 3:5). The names of the unrepentant will not be on the list. 'Guilty' will be their only plea. The Judge will have no option but to banish them from his presence forever to the place the Bible calls hell (Matt. 5:22).

You will find that most people today reject this kind of teaching, but their only reason is that they do not like it. Millions delude themselves with the idea that since God is good, hell cannot exist. Conveniently, hell, for most of them is a state of mind. The notion of a place of punishment does not fit in with their idea of a loving God. They do not realise that to entertain such ideas is to abuse God's goodness and to aggravate their guilt. Why would God sacrifice his one and only Son to save sinners if hell were merely an idea?

Do not allow yourself to be influenced by these attitudes. Let me say it again, to make progress in the Christian life you must always be keenly aware of the appalling consequences of unforgiven sin from which you have now been delivered. Obviously, you must not dwell too much on that grim miry pit out of which you have been rescued, but to peer into its depths now and again is a healthy thing to do. It will ensure that your gratitude to God for pulling you out of it never dies.

Paul tells us that God presented Christ 'as the one who would turn aside his wrath, taking away sin through faith in his blood. He did this to demonstrate his justice, because in his forbearance he had left the sins committed beforehand unpunished — he did it to demonstrate his justice at the present time, so as to be just and the one who justifies those who have faith in Jesus' (Rom. 3:25-26). In other words, because turning a blind eye to sin is contrary to divine justice, it was necessary for God publicly to demonstrate his justice in the death of Christ.

Now that the Lord Jesus Christ has taken the punishment for our sin, God is both 'faithful and just' to forgive our sins (1 John 1:9). He is faithful to his promise to forgive all those who call upon him, and he is perfectly just to justify the believing sinner because his debt has been paid.

Those who hope God will simply overlook their sins are vainly hoping that he will be unjust — like a human judge finding a criminal not guilty, knowing that he is. Jesus himself describes the plight of all who refuse to repent, in simple but graphic language: 'Depart from me, you who are cursed, into the eternal fire prepared for the devil and his angels' (Matt. 25:41).

We see then, that it is for their own false comfort that people deny the existence of hell. They get relief from their fears by making fun of it. Jesus, however, will not allow them to escape. Indeed, we learn more about hell from Jesus than anyone else in the Bible.

You should keep in mind, however, that although you will never be condemned to an eternity without Christ, Christians are not exempt from judgment. On the day of God's wrath, he '"will give to each person according to what he has done". To those who by persistence in doing good seek glory, honour and immortality, he will give eternal life. But for those who are self-seeking and who reject the truth and follow evil, there will be wrath and anger' (Rom. 2:6-8). Our status in life will count for nothing. What matters is whether we have obeyed God's law.

But wait! Surely, this is a contradiction. Does the Bible not say we are saved by grace alone? (Eph. 2:8). Yes it does! How then can 'persistence in doing good' count for anything? The reason is this: Righteousness in our lives is the proof of grace in our hearts. We are saved by grace in order to be like Jesus, and if we are not growing into his likeness, we are not saved by grace.

Take my own case. I have been a Christian for sixty-eight years, during which time I have had ample opportunity to prove my faith by the way I live. If, like the dying thief, I had died within an hour or so of my conversion, I would now be safe with Christ (Luke 23:42-43). But if after sixty-nine years I were still a blasphemer, my 'conversion' would prove to be bogus. I could expect nothing but wrath and anger.

You may wonder why Jesus told the dying thief he would go straight to paradise. After all, he was not able to prove to anyone that his faith was genuine. But Jesus did not need proof. He saw into the dying man's heart and on the basis of what he saw, he said, 'today you will be with me in paradise'. God knows whether we are genuine or not.

In chapter two of the Letter to the Romans (quoted above), where Paul speaks about everyone being judged 'according to what he has done', Paul is outlining the general principles on which justice will be administered. The Jews, for example, must not think that their privileged position as God's chosen race will give them some kind of immunity. On the contrary, 'all who sin under the law will be judged by the law' (Rom. 2:12). The dividing line is drawn between those who believe the truth and as a result, persist in doing good and those who reject it and do evil.

Therefore, when we appear at the judgment seat of Christ every one of us will 'receive what is due to him for the things done while in the body' (2 Cor. 5:10). Since Paul includes himself in this statement, it is clear that this judgment applies to all Christians. On that day, there can be no pretence and no cover-up because nothing can be hidden from God. The believer who has failed to build on his faith in Jesus Christ will suffer loss although 'he himself will be saved, but only as one escaping through the flames' (1 Cor. 3:15).

Those who do not know God however, and do not obey the gospel of our Lord Jesus, 'will be punished with everlasting destruction and shut out from the presence of the Lord and from the majesty of his power on the day he comes to be glorified in his holy people...' (2 Thess.1:9-10).

*Just as man is destined to die once,*
*and after that to face judgment,*
*so Christ was sacrificed once*
*to take away the sins of many people...'*
*(Heb. 9:27-28)*

# STEP 5:
# BELIEVE IN JESUS

*'Salvation is found in no-one else,*
*for there is no other name under heaven given to men*
*by which we must be saved'*
*(Acts 4:12)*

Jesus is very precious to God the Father. He is God's eternal
and beloved Son, and the one who accomplished our redemption. For this reason, God 'gave him the name that is above
every name' (Phil. 2:9).

He is very precious to believers too, because he is our
Saviour and Lord. When we turn from our sins, and put our
trust in him, God gives us his Holy Spirit by whom we are
born into God's family. In this way, God becomes our Father
and Jesus our brother.

You will avoid many pitfalls if you realise early in your
Christian life that you cannot take any credit for your conversion. If you become a serious student of the Scriptures, as you
should, you will discover that by drawing you to himself, God
was following his eternal plan.

As the Judge of all the earth, all whom he calls he reckons
as righteous in his sight because Christ has taken the penalty for
their sins. This is known as being justified.

Having begun a good work in you, he will not forsake you.
He will finish the work he has begun and bring you safely to
glory (Phil. 1:6). You are secure in his love.

# Who Is Jesus?

*'For to us a child is born, to us a son is given,*
*and the government will be on his shoulders.*
*And he will be called Wonderful Counsellor, Mighty God,*
*Everlasting Father, Prince of Peace'*
*(Isa. 9:6)*

The apostle Peter refers to Jesus as a precious stone. He says
that the stone is precious to God and precious to those who
believe (1 Peter 2:4-7). But he is not comparing Jesus to a precious jewel, say, like a diamond. The preciousness of the Son
of God cannot be compared to a million finest diamonds. Peter
is thinking of a building in which Jesus is the living main corner stone holding the building together, and all the other living
stones are Christian believers.

Why then is Jesus so precious? He is precious to God because he is the Father's eternal and beloved Son. More than
that, God is so pleased with Christ's perfect life and sacrificial
death that he raised him to the highest place in the universe and
gave him the name that is above every name (Phil. 2:9).

Jesus is precious to believers because as a man, he is our
brother (Heb. 2:11-12) and our Saviour. He who created the universe (John 1:3) 'became flesh and made his dwelling among us'
(John 1:14). He who is 'the radiance of God's glory and the exact
representation of his being' (Heb. 1:3) has made God known to
us. He who is without beginning or ending was crucified for us
(1 Cor. 1:23). He whom God raised from the dead is now 'at the
right hand of God and is also interceding for us' (Rom. 8:34).

Precious Jesus is our example too because he is the only
one who 'committed no sin, and no deceit was found in his
mouth' (1 Peter 2:22). Not only so, he is also the one into whose
perfect likeness we shall one day be transformed (1 John 3:2).
Indeed, this is the reason why God saved us. He predestined us
'to be conformed to the likeness of his Son' (Rom. 8:29). What

more glorious prospect could there be? We shall come back to this in the next section.

The Gospels give clear evidence of the divine and human natures of Christ, united in one Personality. We see him controlling the wind and the waves, walking on the water, and raising the dead. We also see him sitting on a well because he was tired, weeping at the tomb of Lazarus, and finally submitting to his own death.

His birth too was a miracle. His mother Mary became pregnant during what we would call the engagement, which for the Jews was legally binding, although the marriage had not yet been consummated. Mary's husband Joseph, who was a righteous man, was so shocked when he discovered Mary was pregnant that he needed a message from God to stop him divorcing her (Matt. 1:18-21). He was told that what was conceived in her was from the Holy Spirit (Matt. 1:20).

To unbelievers Jesus means little or nothing. At best, he is a superman and, at worst, an object of scorn and ridicule. His name is used in blasphemy, not only in private conversation, but also on television and radio. Peter also tells us that Jesus, the 'living stone', is 'a stone that causes men to stumble and a rock that makes them fall. They stumble because they disobey the message — which is also what they were destined for' (1 Peter 2:8).

Jesus himself also talked about the main corner stone. 'Everyone who falls on that stone', he said, 'will be broken to pieces, but he on whom it falls will be crushed' (Luke 20:18. See Isa. 8:14-15). This seems to mean that the lives of those who refuse to believe in Christ now will have no useful purpose, and at the Day of Judgment Christ himself will heavily punish them.

That building Peter is talking about is a picture of the true church of Jesus Christ. Believers are joined to Christ just as the stones of a building are linked to the corner stone. We are like living stones built into the same 'spiritual house' as Jesus the living Stone. That is to say, we, being God's chosen, are now members of his church — not merely of that church on the corner of the street, but of the true church of Christ universal. (The apostle probably used the metaphor of the stone because the name 'Peter' means 'a stone'.)

Jesus is coming again in glory to judge the world (Matt. 25:31). On that great day, every created being will bow before him and publicly acknowledge that 'Jesus Christ is Lord' (Phil. 2:9-11). On that day, he will 'be glorified in his holy people'. Their salvation will then be brought to completion (1 John 3:2). The kingdom of the world will 'become the kingdom of our Lord and of his Christ, and he will reign for ever and ever' (Rev. 11:15). He will be 'KING OF KINGS AND LORD OF LORDS' (Rev. 19:16).

Jesus himself will punish with everlasting destruction those who do not know God and do not obey the gospel. He will bring all who reject him to total ruin and banish them from his presence forever (2 Thess. 1:8-10). The prospect is too terrible to contemplate.

You should, therefore, be very clear in your mind that Jesus is not one of many ways to God, but the only way. 'Salvation is found in no-one else, for there is no other name under heaven given to men by which we must be saved' (Acts 4:12). The words of Jesus are engraved in perpetuity: 'I am the way and the truth and the life. No-one comes to the Father except through me' (John 14:6).

Since you now take the Bible to be God's reliable word, you should have no difficulty in embracing these precious truths about Jesus. You may meet people who say they believe the Scriptures but have preconceived ideas about Jesus and deny that he is God. The Jehovah's Witnesses for example, go so far as to publish their own version of the Bible, deliberately altering some words to suit their theories about Jesus.

What you think about Jesus is crucial. As we have seen, God 'has set a day when he will judge the world with justice by the man he has appointed' (Acts 17:31) and that man is Jesus. Your destiny, along with everyone else's, will be determined by your attitude to him. Since he is now your Saviour, you will love and serve him. If that were not the case, he would be your downfall. There is no middle way.

As you go on in the Christian life, you will meet people who claim to be Christians but who have a very different view of Jesus from your own. Like many artists, they paint their own interpretation of what they see. But in this matter we have no artistic licence.

*'I told you that you would die in your sins;*
*if you do not believe that I am the one I claim to be,*
*you will indeed die in your sins'*
*(John 8:24)*

☙

## God's Holy Calling

*'God, who has called you into fellowship*
*with his Son Jesus Christ our Lord, is faithful'*
*(1 Cor. 1:9)*

I am assuming that you have now admitted your guilt in God's sight and have put your trust in the Lord Jesus Christ as the only one who can save you from the consequences of your sin. By the grace of God, you have cleared the hurdle at which many stumble and fall, including many religious people. They fall because their pride will not allow them to face up to God's verdict so plainly set out in the Scriptures and they vainly persist in hoping that God will overlook their sins. Unlike them, you are now highly privileged. If this is not the case, you will need to retrace your steps.

Now you must begin to open your mind to the magnitude of your blessings. Looking back, you should recognise that the progress you have made in your Christian pilgrimage is solely because God has been at work in your life. Do not take any credit to yourself. Precisely what then has God been doing?

The answer to this question is both mind-blowing and heart-warming. God has called you into the fellowship of his Son, the Lord Jesus Christ.

If you ask me why God should have mercy on you and not on others, I simply do not know. Neither does anyone else. What we do know, however, is that you belong to that highly privileged number whom God has given to his Son (John 17:6,9,24). That is to say, God called you in fulfilment of the promise he made to his Son. You are one of the fruits of his redemption.

By the way, you must learn to distinguish between being called and being invited. Everyone who hears the gospel is invited to believe, but you have been called (Matt. 22:14). It was a calling you could not refuse because God opened your eyes to see what was good for you. You chose Christ because he chose you. You must see your willingness to repent and believe the gospel as clear evidence of this.

But what was God's intention in choosing you? The answer to this question is also mind-blowing and heart-warming. The apostle Paul is very clear about the answer: 'For those God foreknew he also predestined to be conformed to the likeness of his Son, that he might be the firstborn among many brothers. And those he predestined, he also called; those he called, he also justified; those he justified, he also glorified' (Rom. 8:29-30). This chain of events — predestined, called, justified and glorified — cannot be broken. We shall look at what it means to be glorified in Step 7.

Believing these glorious truths at an early stage in your Christian life is important for several reasons. First, it will ensure that you give all the glory to God for his grace and mercy towards you. Second, it will keep you from the appalling sin of spiritual pride — taking credit for what God has done. Third, it will help you grow in confidence 'that he who began a good work in you will carry it on to completion until the day of Christ Jesus' (Phil. 1:6). Fourth, it will spur you on to live for the glory of God. For God 'has saved us and called us to a holy life —

not because of anything we have done but because of his own purpose and grace' (2 Tim. 1:9).

But holiness is not stuffiness, and separation is not isolation. God has called you to be separate from the world, and to be salt and light in the world (Mat. 5:13-14). You are to help preserve what is good in society and add flavour to living! You are also to show the way to those who walk in darkness.

*'Therefore, holy brothers,*
*who share in the heavenly calling,*
*fix your thoughts on Jesus…'*
*(Heb. 3:1)*

ॐ

## Justification by Faith

*'Therefore, since we have been justified through faith,*
*we have peace with God through our Lord Jesus Christ,*
*through whom we have gained access by faith*
*into this grace in which we now stand'*
*(Rom. 5:1-2)*

The spiritual loss suffered by many believers through ignorance of this subject is incalculable. Do not let it happen to you. Be determined to understand early in your Christian life how God was able to bring you into a right relationship with himself. Always remember that truth in the mind brings joy to the soul.

This is especially true of the Bible teaching on justification by faith. A thorough grasp of the doctrine will broaden your mind on great themes like the justice, holiness and the mercy of God. It will help you to get a balanced view of the love of God and what it cost him to make you acceptable to him. You will discover that it was not by moderating his standard of justice or by ignoring your sins or by setting your 'good' deeds against your bad ones, as many think. Even the 'good' things we do fall far short of his standard. It was because Christ paid your penalty in full.

In turn, contemplating this great theme will help you to realise the magnitude of the price paid for your redemption. You will begin to see that the sinless Son of God became your Substitute. Your sins are reckoned as his, and his perfect righteousness is reckoned as yours. The prophet Isaiah puts it beautifully: 'He was pierced for our transgressions, he was crushed for our iniquities ... We all, like sheep, have gone astray, each of us has turned to his own way; and the LORD has laid on him the iniquity of us all' (Isa. 53:5-6).

As we saw earlier, appealing to God for acceptance based on our supposed obedience to his commandments is a fruitless exercise. Remember, the commandments make us conscious of sin. But now, God has made known *his* righteousness, which has nothing whatever to do with our keeping of his commandments. Indeed, he has made known his righteousness precisely because ours is simply not good enough. His perfect righteousness is reckoned as ours when we trust in Christ (Rom. 3:20-22). What amazing grace!

Therefore, a wholehearted trust in Christ's death for your sins is the only basis on which God accepts you as righteous. Unless you are clothed with divine righteousness, he cannot look favourably on you because you have broken his laws and fallen hopelessly short of his demands (Rom. 1:18). Our justification, therefore, is entirely due to God's free and undeserved mercy. We are put right with him freely by his grace 'through the redemption that came by Christ Jesus' (Rom. 3:24). And 'since we have now been justified by his blood, how much more shall we be saved from God's wrath through him!' (Rom. 5:9).

Such is the deceitfulness of sin, the temptation to think that God will look favourably on you because you have 'always done your best' will never be far away. Resist it like the plague. It is just not true. All who depend on their own 'righteousness' are barred from receiving God's.

In passing, I should mention that the standard for those who never heard the commandments will be based on the light they have received. God will not hold them guilty of breaking laws they never knew about. Yet, even by this standard, they will fail the test (Rom. 2:12).

Before we leave this subject, I must clear away a common misunderstanding. When God justifies the wicked, it is a purely legal act — just as a 'not guilty' verdict in a court of law changes nothing except the defendant's legal status. We are not made righteous, but pronounced righteous. However, God does what no human judge can ever do. He gives us his Spirit so that we may able to start being obedient.

*'Blessed is the man whose sin*
*the Lord will never count against him'*
*(Rom. 4:8)*

☞

## The New Birth

*Jesus declared, "I tell you the truth,*
*no-one can see the kingdom of God*
*unless he is born again"'*
*(John 3:3)*

The words 'born again' have been seriously abused in recent years. For example, it is now common to speak of 'born again Christians' as if they were a particular type of Christian among many. As much as many religious people may object however, all true Christians are born again. There is no other variety.

I once heard a preacher tell his congregation that the new birth is necessary for people outside the church who live sinful lives, but not for those who have had a Christian upbringing! But when Jesus stressed the absolute necessity of the new birth, he was talking to a very religious man. 'I tell you the truth,' Jesus said, 'no-one can see the kingdom of God unless he is born again' (John 3:3). Just as we cannot live physically without being born, so we cannot live spiritually without being born again.

The new birth is a permanent change. It is the junction where we leave the road that leads to destruction and join the road that leads to life (Matt. 7:13-14). Evidence of the change is seen in what Paul calls 'the fruit of the Spirit' — love, joy, peace, patience, kindness, goodness, faithfulness, gentleness and self-control (Gal. 5:22) — and in the love believers have for one another (1 John 5:1).

The New Testament describes the new birth in several ways: Peter tells the believers to whom he writes: 'You have been born again, not of perishable seed, but of imperishable, through the living and enduring word of God' (1 Peter 1:23). Paul describes it as a 'new creation' (2 Cor. 5:17). The apostle John tells us that believers are 'born not of natural descent, nor of human decision or a husband's will, but born of God' (John 1:13).

The new birth is exclusively the work of God the Holy Spirit. May I warn you again against the widespread error that God renews our hearts because we took the initiative? If this were true, God's purpose in redemption would be completely demolished. Control would be taken out of his hands and put into the hands of men.

When you were born, you were helpless. You may have caused a lot of pain and excitement, but you did not choose to be born. Because of this, when you speak of your birth, you have to say 'I *was* born' because you were passive in the entire process. You cannot say 'I birthed myself'. The same is true of the new birth.

For believers who are not well taught however, it is all too easy to make the mistake of thinking that the change brought about by the new birth dates back to their decision to choose Christ and no further. They routinely assume that because they did the repenting and the believing, God rewarded them with new life. Unless they see their error, they will forfeit many blessings, not least their assurance of eternal life. Make no mistake; we were born of God because he set his love upon us long before we ever heard the gospel.

Another error that has done much harm is the belief that conversion must be sudden in order to be valid. If your experience of the new birth was sudden like mine, you may be in danger of thinking that this must be the case for everyone. I can remember the exact day and the exact time of my conversion. Without reservation, I can sing the words of the old hymn: 'O happy day, that fixed my choice on Thee my Saviour and my God'. Because of this, I made this mistake in my early Christian life. I really doubted the genuineness of the conversion of anyone who could not name the date.

Some time later, I met people who had no idea when the miracle took place in their lives, and yet all the marks of the new birth were plain to see. They were spiritually alive, they loved the word, they rejoiced in fellowship and they were concerned for others. I also began to realise that God had been at work in my life long before the happy day dawned, and that the time it takes is not important. After all, when a child is born, the relevant question is not 'how long was the mother in labour?' but 'is the child alive and well?'

You should also be wary of those who insist on a further experience of the Spirit without which, they claim, the new birth is incomplete. Some call it the 'baptism of the Holy Spirit'. Do not let these people disqualify you. Paul makes it clear that 'if anyone does not have the Spirit of Christ, he does not belong to Christ' (Rom. 8:9) and that 'we were all baptised by one Spirit into one body' (1 Cor. 12:13).

Peter's words should end all controversy: 'His divine power has given us everything we need for life and godliness through our knowledge of him who called us by his own glory and goodness. Through these he has given us his very great and precious promises, so that through them you may participate in the divine nature and escape the corruption in the world caused by evil desires' (2 Peter 1:3-4).

Finally, God's gift of a new heart is the particular blessing of the New Covenant, as the prophets predicted: 'I will put my laws in their minds and write it on their hearts' (Jer. 31:33). 'I will give you a new heart ... And I will put my Spirit in you and move you to follow my decrees and be careful to keep my laws' (Ezek. 36:26-27). Even so, we cannot assume that the experience was unknown in the Old Testament. We read of many people, too numerous to mention, whose lives were shining examples of godliness and who, like us, were saved by grace, not by deeds.

*'For you have been born again, not of perishable seed,
but of imperishable, through the living
and enduring word of God'
(1 Peter 1:23)*

⁓

## Walking with Jesus

*'Do not let your hearts be troubled.
Trust in God; trust also in me'
(John 14:1)*

I once knew an elderly man who, for most of his life believed in God, but refused to have anything to do with Jesus. He regarded Jesus as an unnecessary complication! Since salvation is found in no-one else (Acts 4:12), this is the height of folly. Jesus himself said, 'I am the way and the truth and the life. No-one comes to the Father except through me' (John 14:6). 'Whoever believes in the Son has eternal life, but whoever rejects the Son will not see life, for God's wrath remains on him' (John 3:36).

We cannot have faith in God the Father without also having faith in God the Son.

To trust in Jesus is to trust in God. We make no distinction between the two. Christians love to speak of Jesus because he is the one who came down from heaven to accomplish our redemption. He is the one who conquered death and now, as our great High Priest, he is sitting at God's right hand interceding for us. For this reason we have no further need for sacrificing priests. God has exalted our High Priest to the highest place (Phil. 2:9; Heb. 4:14).

As we saw in Step 2, your trust in Jesus should increase as time goes by. The more we get to know a trustworthy person, the more we trust him. So it is with our God. You must learn to trust him, not only for what he has done to achieve your salvation, but also to guide and teach you day by day. He has promised never to leave you (Matt. 28:20). He has promised to guide you into all the truth by the Holy Spirit whom he has given to you (John 16:13). He has promised to keep you from falling, and to present you before his glorious presence without fault and with great joy (Jude 24). Rely on him totally to keep his promises.

You will have noticed that earlier I said you could do nothing towards your new birth, but now I am urging you to do everything you can to make progress in the Christian life. Why am I doing this? Self-effort before you were born again achieved nothing. But now you have the gift of the Spirit and you must, with his help, do everything you can to improve your daily walk with God. The apostle Peter provides a list of virtues you must add to your faith: goodness, knowledge, self-control, perseverance, godliness, brotherly kindness and love (2 Peter 1:5). This will involve effort on your part.

You will also be called on to suffer so that your faith may be tested and proved. You will have to endure physical illness, disability and accident in common with everyone else in this world. The necessity of suffering may come as a surprise and you may wonder how it can strengthen your faith. The reason is that, for those who belong to Christ, these experiences are a refining process.

But there is another kind of suffering to which every believer is called and unbelievers know nothing about. You will be privileged to share in the sufferings of Christ! No, I do not mean that you will suffer in order to satisfy the demands of God's justice. Jesus did all that for you. Suffering is the pathway to glory for the Christian just as it was for Christ. We are 'heirs of God and co-heirs with Christ, if indeed we share in his sufferings in order that we may also share in his glory' (Rom. 8:17).

According to the apostle Peter, suffering comes 'so that your faith — of greater worth than gold, which perishes even though refined by fire — may be proved genuine and may result in praise, glory and honour when Jesus Christ is revealed' (1 Peter 1:7). The attitude of a hostile world will be one cause. 'In fact,' says Paul, 'everyone who wants to live a godly life in Christ Jesus will be persecuted' (2 Tim. 3:12).

Again, the writer to the Hebrews informs us that hardship is a discipline from God. You are called to endure it because 'God is treating you as sons' and 'God disciplines us for our good, that we may share in his holiness'. It will not be pleasant, but later on it will produce 'a harvest of righteousness and peace for those who have been trained by it' (Heb. 12:7,10,11).

Above all, remember that Jesus was tempted in every way just as we are — yet without sin. There is no part of your suffering which he does not understand. And so, he is able to sympathise with you in your weaknesses (Heb. 4:15). So, when testing comes, lean hard on him, for he has promised not to let you be tempted beyond what you can bear (1 Cor. 10:13). Even if the power of the temptation comes as a total surprise and is much stronger than you thought possible, by his grace you will be able to triumph over it.

There may be times when you will be called to trust where you cannot see — when you are unable to trace God's hand in your trial. At these times you may feel as though he has forsaken you. But he has promised never to forsake you and he is true to his word. God expects you to trust in him at these times too. Again, later on, you will discover that you learned precious lessons as you passed through the dark tunnel, lessons that could not have been learned any other way.

Part of your privilege and duty as a believer is to be a witness to your Saviour. As Jesus said, 'let your light shine before men, that they may see your good deeds and praise your Father in Heaven' (Matt. 5:16). A profession of faith is very important as Paul explains: 'if you confess with your mouth "Jesus is Lord," and believe in your heart that God raised him from the dead, you will be saved. For it is with your heart that you believe and are justified, and it is with your mouth that you confess and are saved (Rom. 10:9-10).* Do not try to be a "secret Christian".

Finally, be much in prayer so that you will discern God's will for your life. God, having made you what you are, has work for you to do. The apostle Paul tells us that we are not only God's workmanship, but that he has also prepared in advance good deeds for each of us to do (Eph. 2:10).

Most of the guidance you will need for this is in God's word. On some personal issues, as I mentioned earlier, the Scriptures will only give you guiding principles. Questions like 'How shall I use my time and talents for the Lord?' 'Whom shall I marry?' and 'Where shall I live?' are only answered by prayer and consultation with older and wiser believers.

---

* Editorial note: Although Christians hold somewhat different opinions on this issue, it is the view of the publishers of this book that such a profession of faith should include baptism as a believer. You should talk about this with the minister of your church (see next chapter).

I could not do better than to quote some graphic verses from the prophecy of Jeremiah: 'Blessed is the man who trusts in the LORD, whose confidence is in him. He will be like a tree planted by the water that sends out its roots by the stream. It does not fear when heat comes; its leaves are always green. It has no worries in a year of drought and never fails to bear fruit' (Jer. 17:7-8).

*'Blessed is the man who makes the LORD his trust'*
*(Ps. 40:4)*

# STEP 6:
# JOIN THE CHURCH

*'Let us not give up meeting together,*
*as some are in the habit of doing,*
*but let us encourage one another —*
*and all the more as you see the Day approaching'*
*(Heb. 10:25)*

Just as a newborn baby depends on mother's milk for healthy growth, so those who are born of the Spirit depend on the pure milk of God's word. The 'milk' is the teaching we receive when the church meets and when we read and ponder the word of God. This is why the early believers 'devoted themselves to the apostles' teaching and to the fellowship, to the breaking of bread and to prayer' (Acts 2:42).

It is possible to be a member of the local church without belonging to Christ. It is not possible however, to belong to Christ without belonging to the church of Christ. God is now your Father and other believers, wherever they live, whatever they are like, are your brothers and sisters. As a member of the church of Christ, you also have a duty to belong to a local church, with all its imperfections.

If you came to know the Lord in the church you attended, you may be spared the onerous task of finding a suitable one. But if you were converted outside the church, perhaps by reading the Bible or talking to someone, it may be difficult to find a venue where the word of God is faithfully preached.

Fellowship with the Lord's people means helping and encouraging one another. It means talking together about our precious faith. If you find such a fellowship, treasure it at all costs.

## Which Church?

*'They devoted themselves to the apostles' teaching
and to the fellowship, to the breaking of bread and to prayer'
(Acts 2:42)*

What a tragedy it is when unwanted babies are left in shop doorways or on rubbish heaps. The newborn child cannot fend for himself and needs immediate help. Unless the parents are found or someone is willing to adopt him, he will be passed around from one institution to another. As he grows up, having no family to relate to, he will feel deprived and insecure, especially if he has brothers and sisters but doesn't know where they are.

How much better to be born into a loving family! From the very beginning, the child is cared for. Feeling loved, and having a keen sense of belonging, he feels secure. When he grows up, he is much more likely to be a credit to his parents and to contribute to the well-being of the family.

Although there are notable exceptions, these principles also apply when a person is born again. He has put his trust in Christ, perhaps as a result of reading the Bible or hearing the gospel at some event outside the church, but doesn't know what to do next.

Now I have to be frank here. In the first few months, or even years, the situation may get worse. You may go to the nearest church, thinking that God's children will be found there, but immediately you feel like a fish out of water. Then you go from church to church in the hope of finding fellowship but you are bitterly disappointed with all of them. We know that in some cases it takes years for new converts to find a church where they are warmly welcomed as brothers in Christ.

You will notice that I speak about the church in two ways. First, it is the universal church, the company of all Christian believers throughout the world. God knows who they are. Second, it is the building on the corner of the street, or rather the people who worship in it. In the first case, all who belong to Christ are members. In the second case, the members are written on a roll, many of whom may not be members of the true church of Christ. The word 'church' is also used today to describe a particular organisation or denomination, although you will not find it used that way in the Bible.

Not knowing your circumstances, I cannot tell you which church to attend, but I can give you some advice on how to find the right church. You should realise from the outset that it is a mistake to assume that good preaching and Christian fellowship is to be found in every church. If you are to make good progress, the church you join must be a Bible-based church, if that is humanly possible. That is to say, it must be a church where the Bible is faithfully taught and the gospel faithfully proclaimed.

You should also know that if a church is described as 'evangelical' it does not necessarily mean that it is the right one. Extreme cults use the word to describe themselves nowadays. The best way to find out what a church is like, is to attend the services and talk to the people and perhaps also to the minister.

Sad to say, the state of the church in the United Kingdom today is rather grey, but you must learn to live with it. In some areas, you would find yourself travelling for many miles without finding a single Bible-believing church. After all, Jesus warned us to watch out for false prophets: 'They come to you in sheep's clothing, but inwardly they are ferocious wolves' (Matt. 7:15). Even one of Jesus' disciples turned out to be a traitor. Paul too, warned the church in Ephesus against 'savage wolves' — men who distort the truth — who would come into the church and not spare the flock (Acts 20:29,30). These people are always around.

Thankfully, there are some bright spots. The problem is, however, when you are very young in the faith you may not have sufficient knowledge to distinguish one church from another. But if you are truly born again of the Spirit, you should be able to recognise true fellowship and biblical preaching.

Another problem arises here. You may find yourself living a long way from the church. Even so, if it is not *too* far away, it may well be worth the journey. Commuting long distances to church has its problems, but it is better than belonging to a church that is no more than a religious club or to no church at all.

If you are already settled in a good evangelical church, be thankful for it. In this case, much of what I have said will not apply to you. If, however, you are unable to find the right church, you will be starved of fellowship and will be unable to participate in the fellowship of the Lord's table — the service we call 'Communion', 'the Breaking of Bread', or the Lord's Supper. This would be a great loss. Jesus himself instituted this ordinance, in which we remember his death and look forward to his coming again.

Never give up. As a last resort, if you can find other believers in similar circumstances, try to arrange to meet together in someone's house. If all your efforts fail and you find yourself isolated, the Lord will come to your aid. Read God's word regularly, and pray over what you read. This is important whatever your circumstances, but especially so if you do not have access to teaching or fellowship.

Finally, when you have settled in a church, never allow your absence from worship to become a habit (Heb. 10:25). You cannot expect God to make good the loss if you are frequently absent. Your spiritual growth will suffer.

*'I rejoiced with those who said to me,*
*"Let us go into the house of the LORD"'*
*(Ps. 122:1)*

☙

## Fellowship and Service

*'We proclaim to you what we have seen and heard,
so that you also may have fellowship with us.
And our fellowship is with the Father
and with his Son, Jesus Christ'
(1 John 1:3)*

We learn from the above verse that one of the purposes of pro-claiming the gospel is that those who believe should have fellow-ship together. We sometimes call it horizontal fellowship. The second half of the verse speaks of 'fellowship with the Father and with his Son, Jesus Christ'. This has been called vertical fellowship.

Why should John talk about two kinds of fellowship? Is he saying that apostles are privileged to have the vertical variety but ordinary believers have to be content with the horizontal kind? Not at all. He is saying that true Christian fellowship is *both* horizontal and vertical at the same time, because fellowship with those who are born of the Spirit is also fellowship with the Father and the Son. 'Where two or three come together in my name,' Jesus said, 'there am I with them' (Matt. 18:20).

This is what makes 'fellowship' a special word for Christians. When unbelievers meet together and chat, Christ is not in fel-lowship with them. Strictly speaking, it is not fellowship at all. Unhappily, what many churches call fellowship is often similar — nothing more than a social chitchat. In the Scriptures, 'fellow-ship' always refers to communion with God and with his people.

As you move on in the Christian life, you may meet many people who come to church on Sunday but will not come to the more informal 'fellowship' meetings midweek. They do not want to be involved. But a believer who does not long for fellowship with his brothers and sisters in Christ, is an oddity. He is doing himself an injury by forfeiting the mutual encour-agement and support of his fellow believers. Do not follow his example.

Not that the fellowship of the local church is ever perfect. The perfect church on earth does not exist. Even so, where the fellowship is sweet, it is a foretaste of heaven. One of the reasons for the imperfection is that the old sinful nature is still alive. In addition, the Lord calls people from all walks of life and you may not have a natural liking for some of them. Nevertheless, now that you are a Christian, you are called to love them. This means that you must always be patient. Do not provoke anyone by looking down on them (Gal. 5:26). Rather be ready to help others with their problems if you can, for in this way you will fulfil the law of Christ (Gal. 6:2).

You may also be called to some special task for the Master. When you have found a spiritual home and your circumstances permit, always be open to the possibility. Those who 'can be trusted with very little can also be trusted with much' (Luke 16:10).

My personal experience may help here. Within a few weeks of my conversion, I became aware of a calling to the ministry of the church, but the church to which I belonged would not have been sympathetic. Before my conversion to Christ, the members complained about my bad behaviour, and they were justified in doing so. But when I turned to Christ and my life changed for the better, they still complained. Now I was far too religious! It was not until I was married with a family that the way opened for me. I now look back with gratitude over many years of ministry in the church and thank God for the privilege.

Of course, the Lord deals with us all differently. He may want you to serve him as a plumber or a homemaker. If you should sense that God may be calling you, the secret is to talk to experienced believers and be much in prayer, asking the Lord to make his will known.

In the meantime, 'Always be prepared to give an answer to everyone who asks you to give the reason for the hope that you have' (1 Peter 3:15). Do it graciously when the opportunity arises, even in the early days when you may not feel qualified.

Tell your friends what you know, and if anyone should ask a question that you cannot answer, do not be afraid to say 'I don't know'.

A good example to follow is that of the blind man, whose sight Jesus restored. He was so ignorant, he did not even know whether Jesus was a sinner or not. Yet, when the Pharisees questioned him on the matter, he replied: 'Whether he is a sinner or not, I don't know. One thing I do know. I was blind but now I see!' (John 9:24-25).

*'Every day they continued to meet together in the temple courts.*
*They broke bread in their homes and ate together*
*with glad and sincere hearts, praising God and*
*enjoying the favour of all the people.*
*And the Lord added to their number daily*
*those who were being saved'*
*(Acts 2:46-47)*
ᔓ

## The Ministry of the Word

*'All Scripture is God-breathed and is useful for teaching,*
*rebuking, correcting and training in righteousness,*
*so that the man of God may be thoroughly*
*equipped for every good work'*
*(2 Tim. 3:16-17)*

Just as you needed milk when you were a baby, so now, as a newly born believer, you need teaching. You may recall the apostle Peter's words: 'Like newborn babies, crave pure spiritual milk, so that by it you may grow up in your salvation, now that you have tasted that the Lord is good' (1 Peter 2:2-3). There can be no doubt that Peter is referring to the 'milk of the word' — the sustenance provided by the Scriptures.

The milk you needed as a baby had to be pure. Healthy growth depended on it. By describing the word as '*pure* spiritual milk', Peter is insisting that the teaching of young converts must be free from error because good teaching leads to healthy growth.

'Faith comes through hearing the message,' as Paul explains, 'and the message is heard through the word of Christ' (Rom. 10:17). This means that every person who turns to Christ does so because he has heard and believed the word. He may hear it from a friend or from a preacher. He may 'hear' it through reading. Peter too tells us that we were born again 'through the living and enduring word of God' (1 Peter 1:23). But God not only uses his word to bring us to faith but also to help us grow in the faith. For 'man does not live on bread alone but on every word that comes from the mouth of the LORD' (Deut. 8:3).

I knew a young minister who went to a new church. His first sermon was very short indeed — about ten minutes. Afterwards, one of the church officials made a point of thanking him profusely for the 'good' sermon. Anxious to find out what was so good about it, the young man plied the church official with questions, only to discover that the sermon was considered good because it didn't last long!

This deplorable attitude to preaching is now common. It has happened, not because people cannot concentrate for more than a few minutes as is commonly supposed, (although those who have no interest in God's word may suffer in this way) but because many 'preachers' have lost confidence in the gospel. When that happens, it is inevitable that the people in the pews will lose interest. Indeed, those who are hungry for the word of God will feel deprived and probably go elsewhere.

As I said in the last section, you will soon be able to recognise the difference between churches where this happens, and those where the preaching of the word is a stimulating and instructive part of worship. In these churches, members of the congregation will be eager to learn, so that there is always an air of expectancy when the sermon begins. You will certainly find true believers in such a church because when the Lord's people are hungry, they go to where the food is.

In churches of this calibre, you will find that many of your questions are answered and your problems solved without having to ask anyone. Your heart will be warmed and your mind opened to the glorious privileges that are now yours as a Christian. And it gets better as it goes on. You will discover that, as you grow spiritually, so will your appetite for the word. The sheer delight and satisfaction of hearing the Scriptures faithfully proclaimed will never fade. On the contrary, you will still be taking delight in the ministry of the word when you are old, as I do.

*'I have treasured the words of his mouth*
*more than my daily bread'*
*(Job 23:12)*

# STEP 7:
# LIVE IN THE LIGHT OF GLORY

*'Since, then, you have been raised with Christ, set your hearts
on things above, where Christ is seated at the right hand of God'
(Col. 3:1)*

The best is yet to come. You are on your way to heaven. Your
present sufferings are not worth comparing with the glory that
will be revealed in you (Rom. 8:18). Keep your eyes on Jesus,
seeing him as the risen and ascended Lord, knowing that one day
you will share his glory forever. Even though you see him now
by faith, the prospect of being transformed into his likeness
will fill you with an inexpressible and glorious joy (1 Peter 1:8).

In the meantime, meditate on the cross regularly. The best
time to do this is when you come to the Lord's Table. Resist
the devil. He has no power over you. Stand firm in your faith
(1 Peter 5:8-9). Continue to make every effort to please God in
the way you live. He expects no less. Do not allow unbelievers
to mould your character (Rom. 12:2), but make Jesus your example. And do not forget that you are shielded by God's power
(1 Peter 1:5) and he will bring you safely to glory.

## The Christian's Hope

*'Praise be to the God and Father of our Lord Jesus Christ!
In his great mercy he has given us new birth into a living hope*

*through the resurrection of Jesus Christ from the dead,*
*and into an inheritance that can never perish, spoil or fade —*
*kept in heaven for you...'*
*(1 Peter 1:3-4)*

According to Albert Schweitzer, 'happiness is nothing more than good health and a bad memory'. Presumably, the bad memory is necessary in order to protect the mind from all the sadness and evil of the past. Many people go further and work on the principle that to enjoy themselves they must escape from the mind altogether and the only way to do this is to get blind drunk.

Others, who would not go that far, still think of joy as something that is worked up. They talk of '*making* merry' or '*making* whoopee'. They see the process as a conscious effort to break free for a while from the dull routine of life.

True joy, however, is a quality of life that is grounded in the knowledge of God. It is the precious gift of his Spirit (Gal. 5:22). It affects the emotions but is not merely emotional. It may have its peaks and troughs but it never fades altogether because it does not depend on our circumstances.

Although words are far too inadequate to portray godly joy, the Psalmist provides us with a beautiful description, with emphasis on its never-ending quality: 'You have made known to me the path of life; you will fill me with joy in your presence, with eternal pleasures at your right hand' (Ps. 16:11). The Christian heart thrills with a joy that gets better by the day and will, one day, be perfect and unbroken.

To be walking in 'the path of life' is to live life to the full. It is to walk with God in the way that leads, without interruption, into his glorious presence. As he travels through this troubled world, the Christian will, like his Master, be a man of sorrows, but at the same time he will be able to rejoice as no one else can, because a life of everlasting and pure joy is just round the corner.

Even if you are expecting an inheritance here on earth, be it a mansion in an idyllic setting or billions in cash, do not set your heart on it. It cannot compare with your inheritance in heaven. If you die before your benefactor, these earthly treasures will not be yours anyway. And ultimately, no matter who the owner is, they will perish, along with everything else on this earth (2 Peter 3:10). Material possessions have no permanent value. The joy they provide is flawed and fleeting.

By contrast, your heavenly inheritance 'can never perish, spoil, or fade' (1 Peter 1:4). Unlike earthly possessions, you will never grow tired of it. Nor is there any danger of missing out, because God has reserved it for you, and will shield you until you take possession. You will share it with all those people from every tribe and language and people and nation (Rev. 5:9) who, like yourself, have been redeemed by the precious blood of Christ. The fellowship will be unblemished.

It is important, therefore, to be confident of that glorious future. According to the writer to the Hebrews, 'faith is being sure of what we hope for and certain of what we do not see' (Heb. 11:1). This inner certainty may not be your immediate experience, but it will grow stronger as you walk with the Lord, always providing you do not neglect the means of grace — worship, fellowship, teaching and a habit of studying the Scriptures privately.

Your ability to rejoice will also increase. Since we have been justified by faith, says the apostle, we have peace with God now, 'and we rejoice in the hope of the glory of God' (Rom. 5:1-2). In other words, we not only rejoice in God's present blessings, but in the greater future ones as well.

Your inheritance in heaven will not be an experience without substance. You will not be floating around in the clouds playing your harp all day. You will be enjoying life in 'a new heaven and a new earth, the home of righteousness' (2 Peter 3:13). It may be hard for you to imagine a world in which thieves, muggers, perverts and murderers do not exist, and where there is no greed,

no poverty, no tears and no death, but it is true. Nor is it easy
to visualise a subdued earth in which there are no destructive
storms and violent earthquakes. But God has promised to set
creation free from the curse to which he subjected it (Rom. 8:21).

This long-awaited event of our Lord's return will coincide
with the completed redemption of all God's people *together*
— the moment when we shall all be made perfect. According
to Paul, the earth is crying out for that special day — the day
when God will reveal the identity of all his children and crown
them with glory. On that day, just as God's world will be set
free from decay and frustration, so believers will be set free
from sin and death (Rom. 8:19-21).

Speaking of these future blessings, Paul tells us that at the
resurrection of the dead, our bodies will be fashioned like the
glorious body of the risen Lord Jesus and for this we patiently
wait. For when Christ died for us, he did not only redeem our
souls, but our bodies as well: '...we wait eagerly for our adop-
tion as sons, the redemption of our bodies. For in this hope we
were saved. But hope that is seen is no hope at all. Who hopes
for what he already has? But if we hope for what we do not yet
have, we wait for it patiently' (Rom. 8:23-25; see also Phil. 3:21).
There will be no deepening wrinkles, no failing organs, no pain,
and no funerals (1 Cor. 15:42-44).

We learn from Paul that we have been marked 'with a seal,
the promised Holy Spirit, who is a deposit guaranteeing our
inheritance...' (Eph. 1:13-14). That is to say, the Holy Spirit
within us seals us as God's property so that no power in the
universe can dispossess us.

The greatest joy of all, however, will be to set your eyes on
your greatest treasure — the glorified Lord Jesus. In a flash, the
glorious sight of him will change you forever (1 Cor. 15:51-54).
It is impossible to grasp the splendour of this event, but you
may rest assured that God's purpose to make you like Jesus
will be finally realised (Rom. 8:29). The Spirit's work in you will
then be complete (2 Cor. 3:18).

Death, the final enemy will be conquered. The Lord Christ himself will destroy it. 'For he must reign until he has put all his enemies under his feet. The last enemy to be destroyed is death' (1 Cor. 15:25-26). At present, death always wins, no matter what we do to delay it. The wrinkles get deeper and the teeth fewer, and one by one our friends depart. How depressing it all is! The day is coming however, when the glory of God in us will obliterate the memory of this sad world.

To maintain a healthy state of mind and to maximise your joy then, continue to ponder all God's glorious promises until they are rooted in your being. Be careful not to put your roots down too deeply in this world. You do not belong here any more. This does not mean that you will be living with your head in the clouds. On the contrary, a sure hope will have a powerful influence on the way you live here and now in this sinful world.

*'…and joyfully giving thanks to the Father,*
*who has qualified you to share in the inheritance of the saints*
*in the kingdom of light'*
*(Col. 1:12)*
ৡ

## Live to His Glory

*'Therefore, my dear brothers, stand firm. Let nothing move you.*
*Always give yourselves fully to the work of the Lord,*
*Because you know that your labour in the Lord is not in vain'*
*(1 Cor. 15:58)*

Worldly ambition is a mixed blessing. I think of the people I have known who would stop at nothing in order to get to the top of their profession. Few made it, and some of those who did died young. If they reached old age, they lived in comfort with a good pension for a few years. But what satisfaction did they have at the end of their lives as they looked back over the wasted years? 'What good is it for a man to gain the whole world, yet forfeit his soul?' (Mark 8:36).

Your God-given desire to please him will keep you from wasting your life in this way. Success in the world, except to increase your influence for good, should no longer interest you. To be faithful to the one who called you out of darkness into light must now be your main concern. Such a life *does* have a future. It will not only bring you satisfaction in old age, but a reward in heaven too, just as it did for the apostle. 'I have fought the good fight,' says Paul, 'I have finished the race, I have kept the faith. Now there is in store for me the crown of righteousness, which the Lord, the righteous Judge, will award to me on that day...' (2 Tim. 4:7-8).

Expect life to be tough. Anyone who has served the Lord faithfully over a number of years will tell you that it is not easy. Jesus himself warned us about the attitude of this world towards us: 'If you belonged to the world, it would love you as its own. As it is, you do not belong to the world, but I have chosen you out of the world. That is why the world hates you' (John 15:19).

Remember too that you have an adversary. The Bible tells us that he masquerades as an angel of light (2 Cor. 11:14). But, although he is the prince of this world (John 14:30) for the time being, his days are numbered (1 John 3:8). He will try to tempt you into sin and draw you away from the truth. But you have no need to worry. He can do nothing without divine permission, and God will give you all the strength you need to withstand his assaults (Eph. 6:11).

When you stand firm, the devil will run away. 'Resist the devil,' the apostle James urges, 'and he will flee from you' (James 4:7). If however, you find yourself in a situation where you are exposed to temptation, especially sexual temptation, you must do the running. 'Flee the evil desires of youth,' says Paul to young Timothy, 'and pursue righteousness, faith, love and peace, along with those who call on the Lord out of a pure heart' (2 Tim. 2:22).

Therefore, you must no longer offer the parts your body 'in slavery to impurity and to ever-increasing wickedness' (Rom. 6:19). On the contrary, since your body is now a temple of the Holy Spirit, you must honour God with it. The sexually immoral will not inherit the kingdom of God (1 Cor. 6:9,10,19,20). You will never be satisfied with your service for Christ. Like me, when you reach old age, you will feel that you could have served the Lord a lot better. But rejoice in this — your service will be acceptable to God. The reason is that we offer 'spiritual sacrifices acceptable to God through Jesus Christ' (1 Peter 2:5). If we offered them in our own name, they would certainly not be acceptable. As it is, however, the blood of Christ purifies the offering. As with the Old Testament sacrifices, the deed becomes a 'fragrant offering' — a sacrifice 'pleasing to God' (Rom. 12:1; Phil. 4:18).

Sooner or later, you will meet people who claim to be Christians but whose behaviour is abhorrent. Do not let them influence you. Live in a way that compels people to thank God for you. 'Let your light shine before men, that they may see your good deeds and glorify your Father in heaven' (Matt. 5:16). Put the light on the lamp stand so that it gives light to all who are in the house. Live so that God may take delight in you. 'Always give yourselves fully to the work of the Lord, because you know that your labour in the Lord is not in vain' (1 Cor. 15:58).

The bottom line is this — God is now calling you to live a holy life. Remember that 'without holiness, no-one will see the Lord' (Heb. 12:14). So 'whatever you do, whether in word or deed, do it all in the name of the Lord Jesus, giving thanks to God the Father through him' (Col. 3:17).

After serving the Lord for the past sixty-eight years, I can tell you that, in spite of the hardships, it has been a joy and a privilege. My failings cause me a little grief, but I look back with joy that God should have deigned to use me. I look forward with confidence.

*Therefore, I urge you, brothers, in view of God's mercy,*
*to offer your bodies as living sacrifices, holy and pleasing to God*
*— this is your spiritual act of worship.*
*Do not conform any longer to the pattern of this world...'*
*(Rom. 12:1-2)*

ॐ

## Prepare for Action

*'Prepare your minds for action; be self-controlled;*
*set your hope fully on the grace to be given you*
*when Jesus Christ is revealed'*
*(1 Peter 1:13)*

When I was young in the faith, the Authorised Version of the
Bible was in general use. In Paul's second letter to Timothy, he
gives this advice: 'And the servant of the Lord must not strive'
(2 Tim. 2:24 AV). It means, the servant of the Lord must not
quarrel. But some of my Christian friends thought it meant,
'do not fight against evil, just let God deal with it.' The idea
still survives.

Living in a sinful world with a sinful nature, and facing our
spiritual adversary (1 Peter 5:8) makes each day a constant fight
against temptation, injustice, laziness, immorality and a whole
lot more. Do not expect any relief from the struggle this side of
heaven. You will, of course, find rest and solace in Christ, but
not as a means of escape from the battle.

'Be on your guard,' says Paul, 'stand firm in the faith; be men
of courage; be strong. Do everything in love' (1 Cor. 16:13-14).
And, as Peter says in the text at the beginning of this section,
the best way to serve the Lord is to set your hope on the glory
to come and at the same time roll your sleeves up for work.

The claim that those who have a hope in heaven are of no
earthly use merely exposes the ignorance of those who make

it. They do not know what they are talking about. Preparing for action and setting your hope fully on the glory to come should always happen in tandem. Yes, it is possible to keep your eyes on Jesus and on the ball at the same time! Christian action and Christian hope always belong together.

The same principle applies to the establishment of that personal discipline God expects of you. Keeping an alert mind and a code of conduct. To fix your thoughts on the glorified Christ and be lazy at one and the same time is impossible. As I said earlier, discipline doesn't just happen. It involves effort (2 Peter 1:5-8).

As a good soldier of Christ Jesus, you must be willing to endure hardship (2 Tim. 2:3). You must get rid of any encumbrance and travel light. I do not mean that you should give away all your money and possessions, but that you should not be too attached to them. Rather, you should find ways of using them for the glory of God. The same applies to your hobbies and friendships.

An athlete has three unbreakable rules. First, he must keep slim and fit. This means watching his weight and diet and having strenuous workouts on a daily basis. Second, he must wear short and light clothing so that he is not hindered in the race. Third, he must focus on winning. The rules apply to the Christian life too. The writer to the Hebrews makes the comparison: '...let us throw off everything that hinders and the sin that so easily entangles, and let us run with perseverance the race marked out for us' (Heb. 12:1).

Top runners have the record of past athletes in mind and never tire of trying to improve on them. We have in mind the example of one whose performance we cannot improve on. By example, he teaches us to focus on the joy that will be ours at the end of the race. So 'let us fix our eyes on Jesus, the author and perfector of our faith, who for the joy set before him endured the cross, scorning its shame, and sat down at the right hand of the throne of God' (Heb. 12:2). Just as the glory to come filled his horizon, so it must fill yours.

As a child of God in a hostile world, you will discover that many people despise you, just as they despised Jesus. Do not have any illusions; some you will influence for good; others will hate you. Blind unbelief is not easily shifted. Ponder the words of Jesus to his disciples: 'If the world hates you, 'keep in mind that it hated me first' (John 15:18). The world hates us because the sinful mind is hostile to God (Rom. 8:7), and those who are hostile to God are hostile to God's children as well. If we belonged to the world and did the things the people of the world do, they would love us. But this is no longer the case.

'Finally, be strong in the Lord and in his mighty power. Put on the full armour of God so that you can take your stand against the devil's schemes' (Eph. 6:10-11). Rejoice in this — that Christ will never let you go. You are the Father's precious gift to his beloved Son and no one can snatch you out of his hand (John 10:28-29). Although God expects you to try your best in every circumstance, you may fail at times, but failing is not the same as falling. He may let you fail, but he will never let you fall away altogether (Jude 24).

As time goes by and you learn more about Jesus, he will become more precious to you. Along with an ever-deeper loathing of your sins, the assurance of his love will grow sweeter as the days go by. You will never cease to be amazed at God's love for you. It gets better by the day. Believe me — I have proved it.

*'And now, dear children, continue in him, so that when he appears we may be confident and unashamed before him at his coming'*
*(1 John 2:28)*

## Pray Often

*'Open my eyes that I may see wonderful things in your law'*
*(Ps. 119:18)*

I went to the chemist's to get some medicine for my wife. When I arrived, I had what is often called a senior moment — a time when the mind goes blank. I waited a while to see if I could remember what my wife wanted, but on this occasion, the senior moment became a senior five minutes and it showed every sign of lasting longer. What did I do? I did what most others appear to do in these circumstances. I resorted to my mobile phone.

Every time I walk through a shopping centre I see people talking into their mobile phones. In many cases, it must surely be the novelty of having the ability to talk to someone while on the move. They are probably just chatting to a friend. Nevertheless, the tiny instrument seems to have become indispensable.

When I walk through the shopping centre on my own, or anywhere else for that matter, I am frequently talking to someone, but not on my mobile. When walking on the cliff path near my home I sometimes do this aloud because it helps me to concentrate. Occasionally, people out walking come quietly from behind and must say to themselves, 'What! no mobile phone. Who is he talking to?' They probably think, since I am old, that I am talking to myself.

Some Christians will tell you prayer is easy. It is just like having a mobile phone to talk to a friend. In one sense, they are right. You do not have to use different words from the ones you use every day. And if you have difficulty in saying what you mean, God knows exactly what is in your mind. If you make a mistake and ask for the wrong thing, rest assured that God will amend your prayer so that you only receive what is good for you (Rom. 8:26-27).

Others will tell you that prayer is difficult. In a way, they too are right. We hear of great men of the past who spent long hours in prayer, but when we try to do the same, we quickly run out of words. At least, that is my experience. When you are confronted by a complicated problem, you may have difficulty in knowing what to ask for. And when no answers are forthcoming, you will begin to wonder why. When this happens, be assured of this, that 'If we ask anything according to his will, he hears us' (1 John 5:14).

It is perfectly legitimate for you to pray for your friend who may be suffering from some disease or other, or even for a fine day for your wedding or whatever. In such cases, however, you must always remember that God's will may not be the same as your own. Your friend's suffering may have a purpose, and the local farmer may be praying for rain on your wedding day.

My advice to you is this — make your praying Biblical, asking God to give you understanding every time you read the Scriptures. If you ask for what God promises, you cannot go wrong. When you read a portion of Scripture, try to turn it into prayer for yourself and others. This, in itself, will be a spring-board for action.

When you sin, confess it immediately to God (1 John 1:9). And if, when you do this, you remember that you need to go and see your friend — the one you offended the other day — go and ask for forgiveness. Jesus tells us that if we come to of-fer our gift 'at the altar' (no doubt Jesus had the Old Testament practice in mind) and then remember that our brother has something against us, we must go and sort the matter out first. In these circumstances, God is willing to wait (Matt. 5:23-24).

Finally, do not expect God to forgive you if you do not forgive others (Luke 6:37c). To 'approach the throne of grace with confidence' (Heb. 4:16), you must not harbour grievances against anyone.

*'Now I commit you to God*
*and to the word of his grace, which can build you up*
*and give you an inheritance among all those who are sanctified'*
*(Acts 20:32)*

# Fix your eyes on Jesus
*Frank Allred*

In a day in which many Christians seem to go in for a quick fix spiritually, Frank Allred pleads with us to make every effort to become more aware of the glory of Christ and the privileges that are ours in him. We need also to realise afresh the glorious destiny that awaits us beyond this life – the enjoyment of God's new world in which there is neither sin nor death.

If we would know more of Christ (which is surely the desire of every true believer) we must immerse ourselves in the Bible for therein we shall find every reason to keep our eyes fixed on Jesus.

ISBN: 9780946462650
Grace Publications

# Why I love Jesus:
# a personal testimony

*Frank Allred*

Here is a lively, intensely personal book; compact, yet full of scriptural truth. In 23 short chapters, Frank Allred explains in plain language why he loves Jesus and why we should, too!

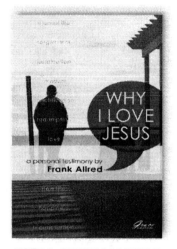

ISBN: 9780946462735
Grace Publications

# Rediscovering God's love
*Frank Allred*

This challenging book, written out of a lifetime of pastoring churches, is a clarion call to rediscover God's love in all its rich dimensions. Frank Allred compares biblical teaching with what is taught in many churches today, showing how far short it falls of the teaching of Scripture. He does not shirk difficult issues, such as how the wrath of God relates to his love for sinners. Nor does he shrink from highlighting what he sees as a sentimentalising of God's love at the expense of his holiness, which results in a departure from the pursuit of vital godliness. The book is in two parts. The first, and larger, part explores what God's love is and how it needs to be discovered afresh in today's church in all its fullness. The second part draws out what loving God means in practice for Christians who seek to follow the teaching of Scripture in every aspect of their lives.

ISBN: 0946462712009
Grace Publications

# Just by believing

## *Frank Allred*

How can I be right with God? Why shouldn't God accept
me on the basis of my own efforts? Surely people were
saved by their works in the days of the Old Testament?
Aren't Paul and James in conflict on this issue? If you want
straightforward answers to questions like these, then this
book by Frank Allred should prove ideal. Although many
people, even within the churches, are hoping that their own
actions will recommend them to God, he shows that this is a
vain hope. Instead, he shows from the bible how we all need
to trust in Jesus Christ, the Saviour who God has provided.
Exploring what it means to have real faith, he demonstrates
that this is the consistent plan of God throughout history
and that, rightly understood, it leads to true freedom and
godly living. Drawing from a lifetime of Christian pastoral
ministry, this book is written in an engaging style and never
fails to challenge.

ISBN: 9780946462759
Grace Publications